# Memories of Texas
# Towns & Cities

# Memories of Texas Towns & Cities

a poetry sequence
by
Dave Oliphant

with illustrations by
Mary Lou Williams

HOST PUBLICATIONS, INC.
AUSTIN, TEXAS

# Other Books by Dave Oliphant

## Poetry

Brands (1972)
Taking Stock (1973)
Lines & Mounds (1976)
Footprints, 1961-1978 (1978)
María's Poems (1987)

## Anthologies

The New Breed: An Anthology of Texas Poets (ed., 1973)
Washing the Cow's Skull / Lavando la calavera de vaca (ed.,
    with Luis Ramos-García, 1981)
Roundup: An Anthology of Texas Poets, 1973-1998 (ed., 1998)

## Translation

Figures of Speech: Poems by Enrique Lihn (1999)

## Criticism

Civilization and Barbarism: A Guide to the Teaching of Latin
    American Literature (1979)
On a High Horse: Views Mostly of Latin American & Texan
    Poetry (1983)

## Music

The Bebop Revolution in Words and Music (ed., 1992)
Texan Jazz (1996)
The Early Swing Era (forthcoming, 2001)

Layout and design: Joe W. Bratcher III

Cover design by Mary Lou Williams

Photograph by Darío Oliphant

Library of Congress Number: 00 132444

ISBN: 0-924047-19-4

# Memories of Texas Towns & Cities

# Acknowledgments

Parts of *Memories of Texas Towns & Cities* first appeared in the following publications, although all sections previously published have since been revised.

*Austin* (Prickly Pear Press, 1985) for Austin
*Brands* (Road Runner Press, 1972) for Beaumont ("Goose Hunting") and Fort Worth (part III, sections 1 & beginning of 4)
*Cedar Rock* for Beaumont ("Class Reunion," sections 1-3, 5-7, 9-16)
*Dactylus* for San Antonio
*The Dirty Goat #11* for Nixon
*Footprints, 1961-1978* (Thorp Springs Press, 1978) for Beaumont ("A Little Something for William Whipple" parts 2 & 3 and "Carroll Black, Author of *Stephen Hero*"), Fort Worth (part IV, section 1), Hebbronville, Laredo, and Wink
*Lines & Mounds* (Thorp Springs Press, 1976) for Dallas, Fort Worth (parts I & VI), Houston, and Vidor
*María's Poems* (Prickly Pear Press, 1987) for Fort Worth (part V), Johnson City, and New Gulf
*New Letters* for Beaumont ("A Little Something for William Whipple" part 1)
*New Texas '95* for Denton
*New Texas '92* for Castroville
*Pax* for Salado
*Riata* for Fort Worth (part II)
*Sleepy Tree Book II* for Honey Island, Kountze, and Sour Lake
*Southwestern American Literature* for Paris, Serbin, and Uvalde
*Taking Stock* (Prickly Pear Press, 1973) for Beaumont ("Jazz God & Freshman English" & "Hustling Shuffleboard With Hearts-&-Flowers Harold") and Fort Worth (part III, sections 2 & conclusion of 4)
*Texas Short Stories & Poems* for Beaumont ("Class Reunion," section 4)
*Thicket* for Beaumont ("Class Reunion," section 8)

## Woodville

the alpha & omega of them all
has wanted to move her china shelf
& to make it fit on the facing wall
will have to saw six inches off

her yellow pine with ring after ring
still holding history in its rich aroma
now muse for how many years    three
it's been since her garage-sale find

from one before the Great War started
Stravinsky is arriving on the FM set
with rumbling timpani & slashing brass
a thunder accompanies the serrated blade

as it rips & tears into & through
all four seasons with their sun & rain
soaked by the rhythmic rise & fall
of that composer's primitive strains

on conducting at the kitchen sink
a dance of adoration    a ritual letting
dust piling on the linoleum floor
spilling as if that virgin's blood

were in innocence to pool once more
or the pungent sap could it pulse again
sticky & smelling of that fictive board
Joe Christmas milled in light of August

in what ground did its roots go down
under what sky did its needles grow
did it share that past of Scouting days
or further back when Wood had fought

Creek & Seminole in a shameful defeat
afterwards to Galveston Bay with wife kids
& 30 slaves    later a hero at Monterrey
elected 2nd governor of the Lone Star State

or when Allan Shivers would hold that post
longest of all    his house still brings them in
to the museum its tour guides recommend
Allow half an hour Attend the Dogwood Fest

Come when the tree's in bloom Hear its lore
How it served for a cross crucified the Lord
blasted by God Almighty so twisted & bent
none could think it meant for lumber again

its red berries standing for oozing drops
from rusty nails leave brownish prints
on the tips of white blossoms' petal skin
or maybe it stood back in the '50s when

would chop up logs for the council seating
reached from the highway by a red clay road
a mile or two before George's namesake town
beside the Chief Drive-In's corrugated fence

under the arch at Camp Urland's entrance
among the fallen cones & sweetgum leaves
where she whose wish is a warm command
sends her gabbler to revisit a defining scene

where that summer job as junior assistant
brought reveille earlier than for all the rest
those took on slowly their handsome tans
instructors of rowing canoeing & rifle range

while with morning noon & evening meals
sorted the silverware    stacked dirty plates
cleaned again the peanut butter & jelly jars
swept mopped & scrubbed the dining hall

sweated from steaming dishwashing machines
after dark losing at poker till all sneaked off
to neck with their dates cabined across the lake
or those from town drove their daddies' cars

cooking outdoors had earned in years before
a merit badge with black kettle stitched in cloth
but recall more that patch could never sew on
would've permitted the learning of secret codes

chants with feathered headdresses & tribal beads
all because even then as one of the chosen few
tapped out & hung with a prickly holly wreath
broke silence in that Order-of-the-Arrow ordeal

but first blindfolded & scratched by undergrowth
led to sleep the night alone    no cot    no bedroll
two matches only    told Build a fire in the morning
Burn the wreath If not    but did & made it through

warned Not a word till six at night or get the boot
assigned to saw up trunks    hack off the branches
the guy in charge the one OA in that Trinity troop
& he was not about to give his rival half a chance

while other tapouts were granted one & even two
on letting a phrase slip when they hadn't meant to
with him    not on your life    asked a fellow scout
if he'd mind passing the axe    got it okay    & good

yelled That's it for you bud Report to the mess hall
found the master over coffee in that gloomy room
confessed Yes have a big mouth Can't keep it shut
Most every time have opened it have tasted foot

& has happened again    when all she wanted was
her shelf cut down & moved to the opposite wall
not running it off with tales from the Piney Woods
jabbering on of ballet or a battle won at such a loss

3

# Wink

bat an eye
& miss its meaning

like dad's advice
to his younger son

who talked of buying
a *Triumph* or such

"why what in hell for?
what would you do tell me

stranded high & dry
no mechanic there understands

or even wants to work on
fancy foreign makes"

wondered why this
insisting so on going

to look for trouble
"it's all over

but mostly where
you can't get to from here

in those parts there *are* no parts
so when that *MG* fails"

his last words of warning
"don't phone me from Wink"

# Vidor

is an upright community among the wilds
hardly noticed from the highway splits it
thick with pines & palmettoes hide motor-
boats banks bars every hell-fire sect

here the civilized & the seedy
are sown together in swampy land
though biblical parables need not apply
sex & religion thriving side by side

holy roller meeting times
divide the rainy weeks
half the days for quoting texts
half for fleshly roller rinks

where electric organs service both
for hymning heaven for limbs' animating
skating couples leaping in rainbow lights
or bowed quaking beneath stained-glass panes

out of sight of traffic's judging eye
the two live on as familiar as Spanish moss
earthy unreal as the region's armadillo who's
armored against fed on a common carnal root

## Uvalde

home of John Nance Garner
to drop a name
Veep dumped by Franklin D.
after serving to '41 from '33

how many unknowns planted trees
said a word no wind can now recall
more to the point than whole libraries
donated but deducted dust & all

in '65 with Dave & Mary Jane
stopped just long enough to buy
those cowboy boots    a pair meant
for stirrups not escalators

signed the check & heard the owner splutter
why Tom Oliphant was in this store
not five minutes ago    any kin    not really
yet the same name as that only brother's

had merely driven through so Hickey could see
how the setting should go in his radio story
along for the ride with him & his Abilene bride
though in retrospect it always comes to more

at the time no governor had appointed the dead
to some committee on something or other
Dolph Briscoe    another disreputable native son
from a long line of getters of graveyard votes

or would Dave find this setting too much of a scene
how much can be made of a half-hour visit
does it have to mean more each time it returns
a dozen years later came through on the way to Del Rio

headed for the promise of a permanent job
home of Jesus' very own voice
of that station of the plastic cross
advertiser of relics out of Chaucer's tales
a prayer cloth signed by the Saviour himself

the hottest place in the state
but Hell too needs a signal
beamed to those are keeping cool
in their private pools thinking
Satan wouldn't dare to swim in here

the caves on the Lower Pecos
dating to B.C. twelve thousand or so
their ten-foot-tall figures animal & human
in Fate-Bell Shelter their mystical shamans
Wolfman Jack broadcasting across the Rio Gran'

taking orders for a commode cover glowed in the dark
"My Jesus has broad shoulders like the highway"
Sul Ross University's branch & the natural springs
mostly ridiculed but couldn't care less came or stayed away
turned it down & drove back through Garner's town

near where the Godfreys were caught
in a flash flood trapped inside their car
rattlers massing at the windshield glass
oozing & squirming right over the top
he it was saved square nails from '88

fastened them for Elisa as a knickknack
to plywood shaped like the Lone Star State
helped build Laredo's International Bridge
ranched near here then moved to the Capital
heard him on the bus & it all came back

connections made though the sense escapes
shamans entranced or slithering snakes
elections lost to ballot boxes stuffed with ghosts
a teaching position untaken & the lessons missed
assignments never received if never given

## Sour Lake

mad at the world
for nothing can even recall
always at those who misunderstood

stomped out of the house
a college dropout at twenty-three
too old still to be running off

yet set on showing them all
would hike by way
of Montana & snow

perspiring then on the Texas coast
or was it Wyoming was headed for
just anywhere west & north

only made it to here some twenty
miles from that Beaumont home
by midnight back in its roses bed

after all those plans for cutting lawns
doing odd jobs from town to town
where friendly folk would welcome

hear this Canterbury tale *astonied*
had made it so far & all alone
then to write from Missoula or Butte

Surprise! arrived in one piece! it's forty below
saw it all on leaving the highway road
entering the brush to camp near water

early enough to take some bearings
to build a summer fire & read Thoreau
*Walden* packed in with the match supply

lasted perhaps an hour past dark
till all but carted off by mosquitoes
then started for the nearest resort

hitched a ride with a hick hot-rodder
cruising with him around this town
hardly rubbed up against the Big Thicket

woods where men have wandered lost
nor ever wanted nor needed return
were never at a loss to see it through

had come to touch
what can't be told
nor would it ever have been believed

that kid no romantic bent on revenge
was out looking to pick up some tits
dropped off by him at the laundromat

to wait there safely in its electric light
afraid to go further & hurting to admit
wasn't staying not even one night

in dejection retracing those easier steps
with a heavy backward shadow
from moonlight through the leaves

then spotted a sign of neon life
"Hayseed Beer & Dance"
heard the amplified boom of a Western band

like a heart alone deep in the woods
the silent drift of russet needles
piling as fears at each hoot or rustle

stood there as the couples drove out & in
asked an older set for a lift to the city
to be let off at sellers of oil well supplies

so relieved to breathe again that refinery air
had had enough of such country fragrance
of a trip to a lake of disillusion

this town could keep its sweetgum ways
its waking to songsters on dogwood limbs
its manna of pine cones & blooming azaleas

# Serbin

the doors to its church
remain unlocked
its ceiling's a
celestial blue

its chandelier electric since
its lamps were emptied of
the kerosene they
used to use

suspended from
a twelve-foot cord
halfway up or down
a golden-winged white dove

its tail feathers all agleam
flies to yet never arrives
at the pulpit level with
a second floor looking down upon

the heads all bowed in prayer
or lifted in song yet never seeing
above & behind the ringed eight-
foot pipes blue gold & white

their sanctuary's organ built
by those like the one last Wend
leads their singing still
by those who came to find

a place to worship & found it here
who brought with them
their first hymnal dated 1574
with notes all diamond-stemmed

for services in their prim
bell tower with its white tin
siding its soaring weather vane
children learning fifty hymns

to retain a Wendish tongue
to restore antiphonal song
the ties between Christ & soul
impressed as stenciled leaves

in orange patterns
on square white pillars
their painted black designs
of circles & featherings

the marble-like swirls echoing
the organist's *schwissenspiels*
weavings round the held whole notes
Bach fussed at for writing those

inherited by these
from Gerhard Kilian
that Leipzig-born tradition
he its great practitioner

of slurs & passing tones
a version of the almighty ground
right out of Mendelssohn's Fifth
a sound as if of morning's light

through the fog of winter
on their trip from Liverpool
survived the cholera even as
through their Singing Society

the Spinning Wheel has
though it turns no more
here or elsewhere
as it did before

## San Antonio

"Every Traveler Needs a Mission"
the clever *Texas Monthly* tour guide reads
then lists & pictures each in turn
first in line as it should be Concepción
followed by the other saintly three

San José    San Juan Capistrano
San Francisco de la Espada    this last the one
have never seen    each a church from 1720 or '31
all built by tribes could only receive
their land & water from a Spanish king

each still holding mass for those live near
though friars & soldiers have long since gone
who prayed under beams of Rosa's Window
or quartered close to the fortress gate
to protect against marauding Comanche raids

driven here first in summer dark
from Fort Worth in '44 to find & see dad off
fed up with bombers on the graveyard shift
had up & quit & though with wife & kids
was subject still to the wartime draft

stretched out in the backseat half asleep
frightened by shadows cast in Forest Park
its limbs of trees at midnight black & tall
as another soldier's wife drove & mother spoke
heard vaguely her talk of daddy's call

awoke to the animal stink of Brackenridge Zoo
to husbands stationed at Fort Sam Houston
had made it together through basic training
find now how it's never done    must start again
weekly for twenty years this marriage rebegun

from the day Beauty's mother held back her tears
holding to one another for reasons half-understood
clearer here on this second honeymoon cannot afford
in a room taken at this cheapest of motel chains
its brown-&-orange bedspread coast to coast the same

yet hold each other closer knowing it more than fate
the kids left with their Texas granny who lives alone
traveled all night to arrive before he'd leave next day
being transferred out to Fort Belvore    perhaps gone
forever   how ever take leave of her   what did he say

barely recall that time at all    his return much more
envied on getting out of class to meet his train
how it moved so slowly    then let off steam
the platform lined with trunks & duffel bags
red caps loading footlockers into yellow cabs

spittooned waiting room where benches filled & emptied
with families let out screams then hugged & kissed
though on his stepping down from a chalk-numbered car
mother swore to him she never would
not until he shaved that ugly moustache off

& while she carried on & turned her face away
would feel his uniform's stiff pant leg
rub his winter overcoat of heavy wool
spot the insignia of his engineering corps
eager to know him & hear how he'd won the war

too young then to take it in
& later would fail to seek him out
to learn what it meant to drill with men
were soon to die or thought they might
in army issues & haircuts all alike

in wonder watched him lather his upper lip
as he first told a story he would tell for years
of his whole outfit to be shipped out    sent overseas
except for him who would happen to look around
for another type of work than policing grounds

14

not to pull latrine or mess hall duty
something more in his printer's line
found an office with a shop behind
volunteered to sweep & pick up trash
then stopped his broom & sneaked out back

cranked up a four-color none could run
outranked but suddenly in big demand
attached to their unit & assigned to teach
the printing of strategic maps for Uncle Sam
while now fingers search a sweeter terrain

reach from head to foot where mouths explore
renew old landscapes at each touching press
embrace's ink    blushes to hear such sensuous talk
a coyness according with her simple dress
becoming to an ample mind can't read enough

yet never shows off    in the light covers up
so hurt by her pushing of this hand away
from the one at times has caused deep pain
taken wrongly as a sign her love had waned
who has proven it true again & again

its hills & valleys they came upon    Stephen Crane:
out of the sea their white & golden banner of Spain
Indians mere dots of black on the vast Texas plain
saw a moving glitter of silver warriors    the long
battle of soldier & priest against barbaric hordes

polished their armor with neatness & skill
at dusk yellow stone towers calling with bells
ruins now besieged by indomitable mesquite
summoned to her through an interview conducted here
on a front porch by the Superintendent of Hebbronville

from there set off on the Mission Trail
would lead to Santiago & down the aisle
the favorite motif of this Chilean muse
who planned this visit to Concepción
where the Reverend Francisco Aponte y Lis

cured chiggers before his death at ninety-three
with olive oil applied at room temperature
whose well nor her inspiration has ever run dry
from the very first unworthy of it & so unearned
other than she only the Service took any interest in

a body & mind so awkward so immature
though on turning twenty-one preinducted the same
bused here for testing & made to stay the night
on an upper bunkbed's mattress sagging & stained
then to be examined next day & declared 1-A

though in the end escaped induction as underweight
when among so many had gone unnoticed
how not by her    a fact later brought to the attention
of the sergeant in charge
let go without a dime ninety miles from home

as dad too had eluded the clutches
of active duty & the line of fire
wonder did he feel as guilty
when others fell in vineyards of Italy & France
as in rice paddies patrolled in Vietnam

or did he side in his unread mind
with the likes of the Alamo's Moses Rose
he a Bartleby type preferring not to fight
in spite of Colonel Travis's heroic plan
for holding out to the very last man

to make like a porcupine huge & terrible
to be swallowed by a Mexican god of war
Bonham twice going out for reinforcements
shot from under him his cream-colored horse
returning both times to face the inevitable

Rose a dogged philosopher of inverted courage
his sudden refusal coming in the face of
a bravery considered supreme as ever    climbed
the wall    then looked back down on all the rest
leaped & lit out for the wilderness

16

to run rather his butcher shop till '42
then in '50 to cross the Cajun border
to meet in Lousiana his natural death
while dad regretted he'd not stayed in
could have retired after twenty years

lucky for these in platooning with her
each reconnaissance a chance to zero in
on a topography whose strategic target is
this lone outpost of mutual defense
sacrifice offered at no command

differences remaining unsettled still
opposites in any barracks on equal terms
daily retrained as the rawest recruits
each rough & bearded caress surrended to
unconditionally accepted by her soft & smooth

## Salado

a tourist stop lives
off what it was
long before the race of man

found its unspoiled bed
written up in travel guides
illustrated with color photographs

a glamorizing of historical facts
how stagecoach & Chisholm Trail
ran right through its scenic view

dusty teams & cattle splashed
a creek would clear & clean itself
offering now nostalgia for

that magic stream
any can imagine wading in
the buffalo drawn by springs

go on growing watercress
picked mornings by a Mexican pair
before the crowds drift in among

the knicknack gifts
herds that drew in turn
tribes to camp along its banks

were followed by
Spain's explorers who gave the name
to shady oaks inviting still

& so have come
to its roadside inn
to spend the night

to escape the kids
& what's routine
miss them after only

a day of sights
houses built in
Greek revival style

slave quarters
& other haunts
transoms porticoes & weathervanes

an "Athens of the South"
with its literary society Texas' first
site today of a "think tank"

hosts the deepest of minds
seeking solutions to war & death
the worst & best have caused

greets a gathering of Scottish clans
& since each needs some group
to come back to

just can't resist
Bluebonnets & Thistles
a shop run by a man & wife

he of Scots descent
she    he says
part Cherokee

specializing in kilts & tartan cloths
find in their official catalog
that Black Watch pattern

then long once more
for an unknown world
wonder how & why all showed up

at this same spot
see in other shops
teddy bears & patchwork quilts

antique glass & pewter ware
Beauty drawn to
a sawed-out cow

on a platform fixed
with roller sets
a bag & teats

though lacks one leather ear
need it like a hole in the head
yet buy it nonetheless

hoping perhaps to half-hear
the squish-squish
of a superior day

ask the man who attends
the Double Eagle Hardware
what on earth

are the roosters for
the ones cut out from tin
hear that attendant say

"it's only what you see
another thing to sell"
a barrel full of nails

one room filled
with poster cars
Packards Chevrolets & early Fords

glass tops taken from pump machines
for Gulf & Texaco gasolines
Gold Dust twins on cleanser ads

grim reminder of a past
though scoured will never fade
has mostly meant

a slower easier way
its records kept in a
Central Texas Area Museum

but find it closed
no hours posted anywhere
other eager vacationers

with cupped hands
all peer in
through grimy windows

to catch a glimpse
of that distant simpler day
the lady across Main Street

on being asked when it opens up
answers "let me know if & when
you ever discover Lucille's in

but I wouldn't get
my hopes up none
if you don't never see it

you won't be missing much
it's like this shop of mine"
with its liveoak growing

in one wall
& out the roof
"I keep it open nine to five

but any time I try to close
people just can't stand
not to see what's here inside

as you can mostly tell
it's not worth writing home about
hardly any that come on in

buy a thing
but still they have to have
their 'look around'"

what all can find
in summer's heat
are shade & water

enough to cool & quench
though yet will still be thirsting
for that life have left behind

& for the one will never lead
unless it's through the tasting of
an oldtime native recipe

nothing real's for sale
& when it comes right down
who would make the trade

22

## Paris

have never traveled to see the Eiffel Tower
nor felt the need to view Wim Wenders' film
as a graduating senior only walked in sewers
hiding in the dark & dank with Jean Valjean

when Mrs. Test-on-the-First-Line-Skip-a-Line
gave no partial credit for half those pages never end
none at all unless read Hugo's whole *misérable* thing
though after high school got through it just the same

came in fact not to want to put it down
wouldn't think to either this Texas town
dreamed of while in exile in Sooner land
where the drinking water could never stand

envisioned this as some green & exotic place
supplied in summer sacred colas half frozen
would feel its magic name on see-through glass
on the bottoms of bottles saved for cashing in

returned the way those memories always did
when every Saturday earned a dollar to spare
from the prescriptions biked or cotton picked
*The Daily Oklahoman* peddled on that Altus square

whether true or false non-fiction or carpet ride
each swallow not so much a secret formula with fizz
but a journey back to origins & to native pride
a taste of what it was to thirst for & forever miss

# Nome

on Highway 90 heading east of Houston
from here China is merely five more miles
from fang-white cold & Klondike gold

a matter of minutes to mandarins clothed
with flame-breathing dragons on brocaded robes
from blizzards & frostbite & blinding light

a few hundred seconds to plum trees' flowering snow
the shortest route for trekking back across
as if by dogsled kayak or on tennis-racket shoes

to fireworks & ink from igloos penguins & cariboo
two continents brought miraculously close
by neighboring communities still breed & grow

brahma & rice along their flat marshy coast
named by those hoping to strike a bonanza here
or who aside from cash crop & cattle would throw

I Ching read tea leaves in cookies their fortunes told
proof of a kind of travel relative or telescoped
at one time bound halfway between on Greyhound

home to write against all odds poems in Beaumont
something right out of Ripley's Believe-It-or-Not
when the scene appeared & rendered a clumsy mess

of an owl driven by rainstorm onto windshield glass
stunned & stuck momently there crushed & bleeding
then brushed off & out of sight by the wiper's pass

any thought obscured by lame & fractured lines
as through the bird's impact that web of cracks
& could clearly see it had happened the same

from seeking to link the distant & distinct
& yet with revelation would never escape
& thanks to such mercurial metaphorical trips

this & every Texas town has suddenly meant

# Nixon

after the patrolman turned his siren on
issued a speeding ticket that fateful day
coming back then from Corpus Christi
that breezy palm-swaying coastal city
thought Here all's wrong by association

remember how he would always say
political positions were offered to him
for the simple reason that he was in
the right spot at just the right time
RN with his own streak of fatalism

recalls a photo sent to a '60 *Time*
of a Karnes City sign on Highway 80
reading Kenedy 7-Nixon 30 yet neither
distance nor direction could make it clear
how each candidate would one day lead

passed through both on coming & going
after the sunbathing down at the beach
was driving from there & heading home
hurrying as if the Capital & Gulf alone
were the only two sights worth seeing

a vacation spoiled with Beauty & the kids
happened before with that three-day cruise
on the U.S.S. Haas a real destroyer escort
snapped in a photo as an Explorer Scout
standing on board at that Port Arthur port

marred not so much from sickness at sea
as it upped & downed rocked & leaned
on waves of unreal blue or opaque green
nor inaccuracy with a Browning automatic
at balloon targets towed in fantail practice

but rather on reaching that longed-for shore
ruined on wading out in its warm soft waters
when up to the chin suddenly surrounded by
transparent bubbles & tentacles' fearful sting
& though untouched a nightmare still recurs

or sucked out & roiled in its recoiling surf
till held close & told Shush it's only a dream
not so with that flashing & revolving light
argued had gone faster on coming downhill
an untraveled route Sunday no traffic in sight

but wrote it up & replied Appeal to the Judge
asked where he was said Twenty miles back
another unnoticed on rushing right through
so determined to contest a damned injustice
would take off work & return on Monday

back to this nowhere to confront Clay Allen
a young J.P. fully amazed had driven so far
then erased the ticket from his computer file
chatting of the documents he hoped to save
letters & maps his kin handed down to him

wondered at his hometown how it ever came
to be saddled with such an infamous name
said Not after him but for a lawyer who lived
in the original settlement prior to its move
to where the railroad was coming through

for shipping chickens by tens of thousands
freighted from their annual Featherfest site
on San Antonio & Gulf's now rusted track
beside the drygood store's brickwall mural
its white rooster big as the coal-burning train

pulls Robert F.'s black & white oval portrait
flanked by U.S. & Texan flags painted banner
announcing above in gold letters town & state
against one ribbon end a windmill & at its feet
an oil well pump humped bison or brahma bull

two longhorns in middle staring straight ahead
sponsors on a scroll beginning with Ernst Food
then American Legion Auxiliary Yoakum Federal
& the nursing home alongside two pecking hens
under them red white & blue sesquicentennial seal

at the bottom a clump of grass or a cactus patch
with 1906 in antique lettering to record the year
transferred to Gonzales County from Guadalupe
little of it learned then but later a month or two
searching through the card catalog now obsolete

though the deathless facts can still draw back
as when first & last names turn out the same
the wife's who also ran & stuck with her man
through secret slush fund the thick & thin of
Hiss Caracas Krushchev & Checkers speech

all Six Crises the hearings held on dirty tricks
the tape gap preying on him both day & night
she expressionless at his side with Julie & Trish
"I'm not a crook" "I have never been a quitter"
a picked over "carcass" resigned or impeached

the other Pat given Ireland as his second handle
born not here but in the Old some miles away
early schooling in Luling a southpaw at baseball
could have played professionally or so they say
had he not chosen peritonitis & infant diarrhea

sawing up of cadavers & gonococcal infection
to pit against poor health as an even greater evil
than poor law enforcement or garbage collection
to attack the rivers & creeks turned open sewers
citizens crowded like cattle into a housing corral

indifference & incompetence & apathy stagnate
converting the Alamo City's salubrious climate
to poverty crime & nation's highest TB death rate
interfered with his Board till he preferred as Chair
resignation to dismissal by that fool of a Mayor

but first a rural child with blacks for his friends
whose African fears later too primitive for him
then through equal rights urged a chance for them
conceiving racism in America a malignant disease
& yet with desegregation by bayonet never agreed

fished in Nash's Creek Smith's & the Guadalupe
sharing in the fragrance of the blood-red phlox
in bed by eight up by four pokeweed for scurvy
avoided leaning too near Credit or Communists
but through Wesley approved of making a profit

her Dicky's motto not to bend with the wind
to follow one's instincts instead of expedience
any politician swayed by polls unworth his pay
to resign from a ticket the same as admittance
the more the risk the more one stands to gain

in Baltimore in December at Johns Hopkins
"8 degrees above zero: too cold for a Texan"
that very year when its county had changed
would turn in his bugs wash out his test tubes
dissect a pig larynx read a Longfellow poem

yearning so for the sight of his prickly pear
contemning on streetcars the Maryland men
who rarely if ever would give up their seats
the women not even returning a simple thanks
to him the debutantes' broad as distasteful too

& at the inaugural ball did she dance to forget
bombings & break-ins plumbers & pay-offs
suspecting the leaks weren't plugged for long
a deep throat hole in the dike not a finger fit
or to savor sweet revenge for their '60 loss

the '69 birthday party she threw for the Duke
when for Ellington's 70th in honoring the man
in hosting that royal American at her gala fete
RN swore none swings more stands higher than
can't it draw off the abscess of that dark deceit

& after presenting him the Medal of Freedom
asked the maestro to play for their 200 guests
among them Eckstine Hines Mulligan Brubeck
Cab J.J. Billy Taylor Urbie Green & Desmond
the composer improvising "Patricia" in tribute

to a First Lady written up as permanent press
antiseptic & instead of his *Satin* a plastic doll
every hair in place no substance all small talk
or turn off voters as he drove for higher office
who said of her was tougher than finest steel

with the dam bursting poised & self-possessed
as whenever around the house he proved inept
would stop a dripping faucet unstick the door
slipcover a ratty sofa hang curtains or drapes
the Beauty also a homemaker extraordinaire

changes the view even more her new red suit
protesters in Caracas spattering it with spittle
as it rained from above dignified & unruffled
at their return he calling for Congress to pass
an Exchange led to discovery of Chile & her

this town linking their passage by United Fruit
New Orleans to Panama in an oil-smelly hold
to how he too failed to take Starlight's advice
her code name bestowed by the Secret Service
fit her he said to a T as it does Beauty likewise

but mostly before his proposal at Dana Point
to the way she had nursed her mother's cancer
& not long after to care for a father's silicosis
then those in Seton Hospital with tuberculosis
in that medical school meanwhile under Osler

Pat Ireland would observe a colon hypertrophied
& catch from "the greatest physician ever lived"
that famed professor's infectious love of history
Sir William's precept on preventive oral hygiene
see it each visit to Latimer to have them cleaned

31

leading Pat to read & write the medicinal story
of his own home state from Indian plant-lore
to B.E. Hadra's signpost use of a microscope
on his 1874 lesions of vagina & pelvic floor
to TMA rejecting in '52 Negro membership

in '56 as president gave his inaugural address
on how with Cabeza de Vaca all surgery began
his first operation had made him a deified man
with the arrowhead dug from an Indian's chest
at the sacred center of many a festivity & dance

would record too the Tolchas' goat marrow salve
rolling of cripples in the Rio Bravo's warm sands
massaging exercising applying hot baths & packs
till Major Porfirio Zamora could scratch his neck
a century ahead of Kenney all the paralysis gone

not that conditions or care were close to the best
with no physician about anyone handy had to do
for months Parker begged them Take off my leg
said once he went didn't want it going along too
Bostick would use a dull saw & Kuykendall sew

till he trembled then Burnam took over & plied
a hot needle while Williams his rope a tourniquet
cut flesh with a shoe knife Bostick hacking bone
Parker resting easy a while but then complained
his heel hurt on the other foot & soon after died

or down from Chicago on a duck hunting trip
Nicholas Senn listening with delight to Hadra
his details of the nine new Kraskes he'd done
& when asked what percentage of his patients
recovered from such a treatment said not a one

Melville knew & in *Mardi* tells a matching tale
of a diver swims from a shark & rams his head
on a coral reef his splintered & fractured skull
fitted up with a fragment from a coconut shell
the surgeon so admired though the diver dead

Carboneau should have read Pat on E.J. Beall
who in 1886 removed breast & axillary glands
urged quick action A lump is potential trouble
said Tumor can unnerve the strongest woman
No matter the nature do your diagnostics later

when surgeon nor radiologist detected a cancer
Winsett's second opinion caught it & saved her
Turner doing reconstruction a West Texan pair
then Costanzi with his chemo & sense of humor
after its loss brought back the touch of her hair

Bill Brooke with boyish looks & bedside manner
warm unhurried a native too a speaker of Spanish
knows his stuff but if in doubt always he defers to
his otolaryngologist or Jay Hendrix dermatologist
who excised at last the wall of that recurrent cyst

from attending too closely to an afflicted lunger
Pat's fellow students feared they'd contract TB
some on breaking down withdrew temporarily
he distressed more by being separated from her
his lovely Olive in Mineola missed lips & figure

but felt it best that summer he study obstetrics
winter at a psychiatric clinic of Sheppard-Pratt
where an attorney served as Confederate courier
a victim of spells told of a toe he'd lost in battle
a friend remarking it had been a *notorious* affair

a comedic tale to be set against Chancellorsville
Stonewall's final hours as the gangrene spread
or when Pat's turn came for a drawing of blood
had dreaded that first operation yet going ahead
injected the cocaine & removed an epithelioma

or later his loss of a patient to liver carcinoma
a hopeless case from the start yet painful to face
disagreed with a ward doctor & firmly believed
contributory condition a coexisting pneumonia
his diagnosis proved by the post mortem exam

through it all was learning to use head & hand
from Finney the importance of what not to do
to perform under Will Mayo an hysterectomy
while even with hard times his mother to send
five dollars as slowly his self-confidence grew

then had his diploma duly signed by the Dean
afterwards to serve an internship & residency
before returning to the one he depended upon
for success ever giving his Olive the credit due
in these & the María Poems the central theme

& again the coign of vantage an unlikely town
its rails connecting points north west east south
Yorba Linda to Russia Venezuela China & Perú
Baird where grandfather had switched for T & P
Dr. Griggs delivering dad & in '17 cured the flu

when of thousands dying the patients in his care
were through a concocted prescription far fewer
& over the telephone would even give it away
in line with Doc Matchett's call for each locale
to look to itself for the cause of a yellow fever

not to blame distant lands or a foreign invader
in Galveston Greenville Dowell the first ever
to propose the mosquito as the culprit carrier
in Houston D.F. Stuart said A yankee remedy
for a Texan ailment's too unsettled & vague

said Gather roots & herbs from a nearby grave
Pat reporting on the frequent reckless abandon
of ovaries removed through a Battey operation
Paine saying aspirants for gynaecological fame
showed them like scalps of pale-faced victims

opposed the irresponsible midwifery practice
in Dallas mother delivered by C.M. Grigsby
& in Cowtown both her sons by O.R. Grogan
remember twice going to his downtown office
high in the Medical Arts Building of '27 brick

in '73 with implosion its roof turned elevator
hurtled to the ground unstopping at any floor
carrying all 18 with it & crashing them down
reducing each to an unreusable pile of rubble
though by a dislocated thumb is standing still

had jabbed it grabbing at some mongrel dog
was touching the upper wrist had bent so far
he a large man lifted himself up off the floor
straining to pop the bone back into the joint
& when he did kicked him right in the groin

saw that anger as the first professional fall
of a calm gentle physician had lost control
had earlier taken out those infected tonsils
there on his same stirruped examining table
see that ether-dripped mask descending still

to a dream of two rabbits chase one another
for days after urping from anesthesia so vile
but on awaking groggy & nauseated recall
was given the choice of riding home either
by ambulance or Granny Polk's Oldsmobile

preferred the familiar to any strange adventure
a pattern set until would luckily break it for her
these the attending angels have brought each here
at their mercy for the fixing up & the keeping fit
five surgeries with Grogan's to remove or repair

an appendectomy in Beaumont followed a hike
to fulfill a required merit badge for Star or Life
made it for 15 miles but then returned in the car
admitted to Baptist Hospital at 11th & College
reminded of a deeper debt by this incision scar

of a haunting double room shared with yokels
an injured logger & family from Piney Woods
his tractioned leg in a cast itching night & day
with nurses not looking would smuggle him in
the greasy foods his diet had strictly forbidden

could hardly sleep for all the noise they made
behaved as if they hadn't been in a city before
at every hour talking loud & laughing at jokes
had already been layed up for a month or more
his break wouldn't heal & thought No wonder

felt resentful at first then remorseful to hear
their memories of home & missing of meals
to learn how closely knit those people lived
yearning for their sourbelly & sawdust smells
father mother three sons vs. institutional rules

in Port Arthur Joe Adams removed the warts
then daily feared the painful soaking of fingers
knuckles with such fine lines forever deformed
yet was shut of a shame had covered up hands
& were made less undeserving of holding hers

daddy knew a man over in Liberty or Dayton
who by pointing could make them to disappear
worked for him yet never tried o ye of little faith
later to read with George from his Mary Baker
but found it neither in her Key to the Scriptures

inguinal hernia came of helping friends move
straining with a couch up their apartment stairs
then coughing with a cold discovered the tear
made good as new by Lamar Jones said Don't lift
Don't drive that '68 Volkswagen standard shift

was more afraid then would never come out
from under the effects of that unnatural sleep
the risk of sodium thiopental injected in veins
could affect the brain & cause a memory loss
feared most not to finish the poem on Austin

the worst of all resulting as Burton has said
in *The Anatomy* Pat I. recommended be read
carefully along with Bible & *Religio Medici*
from being a fool most frequent of maladies
to Robert no remedy existing except to cease

this the case of the Texas poet lost his voice
ruptured a blood vessel in his left vocal cord
from yelling & screaming at his placid muse
aside from women in labor can never excuse
to her being made speechless a poetic justice

called for a procedure would shave the nodule
had formed on that wondrous harp-like tissue
of striated flesh vibrated by the passage of air
had left him with a much reduced native drawl
unprojecting as before yet the accent still there

signed the release form for a punctured lung
should Jim Kemper reach too far in the mouth
on pressing a microscope down on the tongue
inserted for magnifying & slicing that growth
to send it off & find what the biopsy showed

squamous dysplasia in the pathology report
& though benign yet still seemed emblematic
of the poet's own breath in hampered form
his instrument afflicted by utterance so rash
had distorted the music at its tonal source

& while silence imposed for four long days
communicating even so with paper & pen
nonetheless with little or nothing to say
no real loss for those unbothered to read
only he feeling for his words a direst need

not alone recuperate these of a private past
but those from nursery rhymes read at night
or those of a Wordsworth meet on every side
as waters his bent old man stirred at his feet
in search on moors for the dwindling leech

or the remedy Piers Plowman found the best
who explains how a Poverty borne patiently
is a hateful benefit protection against excess
mother of health a singer on meeting a thief
lothe to Pride yet a sweet drink to Sobriety

or Chaucer's leche lik noon in al this world
who koude speke of phisik and of surgerye
wel knew he the cause of everich maladye
if it were hoot or coold or moyste or drye
greet harm it was he lovede gold in special

Faustus signing in blood to Mephistopheles
for alchemy & the Americas' golden fleece
rejecting all prayer contrition or repentance
trading a body's health & the eternal spirit's
for that face had launched a thousand ships

Milton's Samson blinded by Dalila's wiles
viper arriving in Gaza with a perfumed plea
since eyesight's not regained let bygones be
forgive receive her as a tender loving nurse
but sees loss of edenic light his just deserts

& before such Puritan faith did Homer sing
of a triple-barbed shaft Helen's Trojan sent
into a gallant Makháon's plateless shoulder
this Argive son of the great god Aesculapius
knowing bitter yarrow root's healing power

is rescued by Nestor's car for serving again
thanks to Idómeneus urging the horse lord on
shouting above the battle din how any surgeon
at cutting out of arrows & dressing of wounds
is worth more than armies of any other men

& after Troy fell to Akhaian craft & stratagem
Virgil too sang praise for their charms & herbs
though the Roman to sound a more tragic note
for courageous Umbro whose touch could cure
would find his spells no match for Dardan steel

yet Iapyx dearest of all to the sun god Phoebus
to delay his father's death had chosen to learn
than Apollonian gifts of augury archery & lyre
practice rather of this the silent unhonored art
following sick goats seek the dittany of Venus

as unawares he bathes away *pius* Aeneas's pain
inflicted by hissing missile of a hidden assailant
when after all his nostrums & tugging with tongs
have failed to extract the enemy's deadliest dart
the hero's blood holds fast & it drops of its own

while Spenser returned to a genealogy of myth
to discover that learnéd leech damned by Jove
down to Hades for ever daring to patch together
a humpty dumpty Hippolytus dragged to pieces
by the fated horses & Phaedra's incestuous love

then leaning on something more solid like fame
Madame approves with the pharmacist Homais
having faint-hearted Bovary with tenotomy knife
cut fleet Hippolyte's clubfoot & make it straight
despising Charles once Carnivet must amputate

the taliped's screams turning unearthly whinnies
from Kafkan horses shove their heads in windows
spy in the boy's side the wound flowers unheeded
with its wriggling cankers big around as a finger
while no written prescription to rescue poor Rose

yet miss ancient beliefs expect miracles performed
parents telling Matilda the pediatrician won't harm
to open her mouth with groom & he both into rape
pleased to force the spoon down on her picture face
knowing to come back later swears he fears to wait

Dora dragging her hysterical leg in a Freudian case
of smoky kiss & a proposition received at the lake
bring on dreams of fire bed-wetting a jewelry box
the interpretive door sexuality's key alone unlocks
to motives repressed the chronic unconscious wish

from epic or Mother Goose to the allegorical tale
but too find those of Pat Ireland essential as well
of his gall-bladder patient complained of a lump
frankly confessing how in the stitching him up
he had left inside his first & only gauze sponge

how Wilkes of Waco could combine a concern
for every medical man to examine the tongue
feel the pulse & hear with ears the difference
between normal & abnormal thoracic sounds
then handle with skill the innumerable scopes

among them lists stetho oto opthalmo gastro
in '62 hired at Paul's to fit corrective shoes
sprinkle talcum powder for viewing of toes
giving kids room but not too much to grow
laced a pair too tight left a baby's instep red

the mother phoned to complain & later read
Paracelsus on how "sickness lends / An aid"
"can turn even weakness to account" "mind
is nothing but disease / And natural health is
ignorance" never to see Baylor's Brownings

& yet to "turn new knowledge on old events"
Wilkes speaking not alone of diagnostic tools
but with a civic pride of warm artesian wells
of living nearer nature's great watering heart
where geysers gush a godly ambrosian health

of a local factory too for a mechanical picker
for freeing of colored from their cotton fields
& once released would allow them to study
to exercise their glorious & guaranteed vote
raise its value from 50 cents to a 5 dollar note

how disregarding dangers & wearisome miles
by horseback & buggy they'd make their calls
at whatever hour any sleep if caught it at all
on the ground with a blanket & saddle-pillow
for a canopy the domed heavens' starry vigil

Sofie Herzog wearing as her heavy necklace
a string of two dozen slugs extracted by her
James W.'s father in Gonzales in the 1850s
using as an operating table wagon sideboards
found his work safer in the clean out of doors

the phys-historian's odious name needful too
for learning after Ford had granted the pardon
how the other Pat exploded in asking For *what*
how after transfusions for hemorrhaging blood
when RN told her he would never pull through

said You have to make it You mustn't give up
in '52 in that critical campaign she'd said it too
then recovered & later from the threat of a clot
from his phlebitis & bedpans urinals & tubes
measures taken to administer a counter shock

Aitken not holding with a malingering charge
become an invalid & a nearly bankrupt pariah
less indomitable spirits would've lost the will
but with a football philosophy Brennan & her
made a comeback to pass his test of character

at the Great '69 Shootout in the Arkansas hills
(if invasive yet crucial to reassess the rejected)
with Longhorns down to Razorbacks by 14 zip
when they asked at halftime what *he* predicted
declared Texas would win & by one point did

tough guy riverboat gambler of global twisting
with a Frost interview on TV to prove it again
to reiterate the old phrases had worked before
peace with honor law & order the little break-in
well-intentioned but gave his enemies a sword

believed by this at last the boil had been lanced
then chose Hyden for his first public appearance
small Kentucky town had conveniently planned
to name its swimming pool & a new gymnasium
for the exiled hero messiah who had come again

earlier turning down this bears his nazified name
a '54 invitation to visit here Commencement day
from Mrs. Wheat as sponsor of their senior class
replied "I like small towns Would feel at home
Needless to say grateful good wishes Sincerely"

41

& had he come would it have made a difference
could it have cured Gloucester's insomnia curse
the play's best brain from politics of discontent
made him face the corrupt motive & clear intent
of cover-up inconsistency obstruction or worse

have taught him how a cactus can take the heat
can needle yet nourish with pear-shaped fruit
in spite of *espinas* will quench & still perfume
speak brightly with a yellow aromatic bloom
with refreshing green tongue ever tell the truth

emptied his medicine chest of *Ex-Lax Tums*
*Preparation H* his mirror's paranoic reflection
did it change Pat Ireland's tune from his in '52
when he wrote to tell RN of the Texas Nixons
"more eager than ever to claim kinship with you"

then to have it hinted how on the Lowery side
Granny Polk's people were at a distance allied
with RN's Quaker mother's Milhouse bloodline
discovery earthshaking as any wrongful voyages
Columbus ever made to this inexhaustible place

Pat I.'s heathens prescribing nuts insects & roots
tubercled *tunas* with a generous allowance of dirt
for inflammation an arrowhead or scarifying thorn
& for rituals performed to expel maleficent spirits
a sweat-house the likes of August in a Texas town

had they invited Dr. Lawrence A. a black instead
such a rhetorical question is too ironic for words
yet see him after winning his Supreme Court case
or three decades later El Paso's transport service
discontinue its colored section without any fanfare

another physician another Nixon yet never to join
the Association as a member from County or State
in any Democratic Primary Election to participate
born in 1884 to a Chief Steward on grandad's train
a medical man serving from '09 in the desert sand

42

first attending Wiley in his hometown of Marshall
founder Rep. Meshach Roberts beaten by the Klan
Mel Tolson's debate teams defeated Oxford & USC
Lawrence off to Nashville & med school at Meharry
three years before Pat I.'s course in Maryland began

one of only two in the nation would accept his kind
his training paid by tending bar & as Pullman porter
from Chi Town to 'Frisco then with diploma in hand
came on back to a Brazos Valley to open his practice
in Cameron where a girl accuses the shoe-shine man

arrested & in custody for despoiling her then dragged
from his cell by a mob burns him in the public square
where Lawrence hears through his locked office door
those dying cries even as above him a balcony crowd
looks on provided for the occasion with extra chairs

in Douglass's *Narrative* with the alphabet learned
reading reveals his own wretched enslaved condition
yet words seem unable to offer any analeptic to him
in sonnet 118 a purgative for the "maladies unseen"
as to prevent his large whipped for any small offence

in 147 reason with its physic about ready to leave
as the love-sickened self-inflicted incurably Will-
ful diseased desire goes on nursing its pyrexia with
a plague of appetite keeps preserving combustible ill
till in 152 even perjures itself facing an optical truth

in 1878 Swearingen of Austin's fellow physician
honored by him for selfless aid given to victims
the outbreak later in Mississippi first in Memphis
where for weak & dying was a pillar of strength
a fearless guiding light till by fever extinguished

*No sentinels with measured tread*
*No cannon's roar nor bugles' blare*
*A more terrible enemy than even man*
*Moving in doomed places its noiseless battalions*
*Down desolate streets through the poisoned air*

*Where among inhabitants appalled & prostrate*
*By that great unseen unknown destroyer*
*A gallant band worn out but never resting*
*Fell unbending one by one at duty's post*
*Conspicuous the gallant gifted dauntless Manning*

two years before at the TMA meeting in '76
had performed for the cataract in a Negro's eye
a linear incision even as Kirkpatrick deplored
this state operating without any health board
urging its protection against all that afflicts

to work together in spite of position or shade
while Burt would assert their smaller brain
a lack of vital power & nervous endurance
claiming with disease their lower resistance
a lesser lung capacity Satch's trumpet disproves

Weatherford College requiring for admission then
no pending indictment & if had served in the pen
applicant's citizenship a governor must've restored
all regularly educated physicians of moral character
eligible as members in TMA but not them of course

& when Keiller felt learning made all men kin
Clopton would remind him he had not yet been
in the South long enough to appreciate prejudice
Rosser considering mere *man* too broad a term
amended to read except those of a colored race

incarcerated in '63 MLK would reject by letter
the myth of time coursing to an inevitable cure
anesthesia of church windows stained to secure
parishioner & preacher from any urgent justice
a taking instead popular opinion's temperature

with the Reverend hospitalized in Harlem in '58
his life endangered by a vicious stabbing attack
RN praised the Christian spirit he ever displayed
divining in his cause "to which we are dedicated"
his winning against those who oppose & detract

brings to mind that contradictory ulterior trip
to Mao's Great Wall where after 23 centuries
an ancestral art still applies to the ears & feet
its tiny needles for a balancing of yin & yang
to regulate hot-cold flow of the mysterious *Qi*

the trick to retain the opposites time & again
of martial & medicinal calligraphy & wushu
as Mark Salzman in *Iron & Silk* that '91 film
practices ritual swords & strokes of his brush
with black ink firm-light on rice paper sheets

RN's '72 journey a return as if to Hippocrates
his views on the impact on man of food he eats
of wheat mixed with much or with little water
observations symptoms diagnostics remedies
how the strongest can hurt in health or disease

in Greece as in China made more mild & bettered
by contraries combined & purged by the changing
of diet the treating each person as a unique terrain
a garden's delicate ecology must forever maintain
to irrigate cultivate harmony in whatever weather

his aphorism *ars longa vita brevis* how physicians
should do everything proper for making the patient
& attendants work together should look to a season
& country to discover the curative thing to be done
the dangers of a restorative course if in the extreme

while Galen the wonder-worker declared nutrition
an alteration of intake nothing pertains to the soul
fiber turning to plasma when digested & absorbed
the vein acting as faculty & the stomach the same
an underlying substance generating nerve & bone

later at sixteen Avicenna finding this science easy
physicians but rulers of health in a physical realm
mastered it & moved on to Aristotle's philosophy
comments on Poetics remarks on Islamic allegory
titled poets the word princes in his medicine poem

then Ibn An-Nafis declared him wrong even before
Servetus burned by the church for writing it flowed
from right to left & through the lungs a happy guess
yet still he failed to advance further the explanation
since his religion prevented any dissecting the dead

till Harvey said circulation when brought to an end
a flux & reflux passing through ventricles & valves
effects the corruption & death of every vital tissue
stoppage of knowledge affects the body politic too
as in planets nature abhors a stationary condition

ducts from the gall-bladder working like conduits
a reminder of Kissinger's first meeting with Chou
James Reston the reporter kept away from Peking
from the most stunning news Tom Wicker knew
to add to Jim's insult acupunctured his appendix

within the web disseminating a moisture & *Qi*
to the organism's every part lung liver spleen
heart kidney the last storing the essence of yin
controls reproduction growth & regeneration
of teeth brain inner ear pupil & lumbar region

at key points a solid sterile stainless-steel pin
for opening in the skin the gates called "men"
that the *Qi* travel as an ancient river or stream
to invigorate a body's vessels glands muscles
to bear sustenance flush hurt through channels

the Pakistani a means for keeping them secret
their negotiations to remove the Taiwan fleet
allies in the extrication from a mired Vietnam
great diplomatic episode of the 20th century
if learned the internal politics a havoc in each

preparing the ground for his operatic arrival
in the libretto's words a *world was listening*
when the orchestra circles & lands his plane
repeating that minimalist yet emotive strain
before the troops march & as a chorus sing

chanting how *the people are the heroes now*
how *the behemoth pulls the peasant's plow*
then high & lower brasses both pound it out
reeds warbling above strings booming below
till history's ears pierced by flutes & piccolo

Alice Goodman's couplets of slanted rhymes
her insert photograph's dark penetrating eyes
with natural stylized rhythms can mesmerize
her lines as needles enter life-force meridians
release opioids into a central nervous system

quackery or cure *intelligence* a *strong poison?*
Chou: *How much of what we did was good?*
& in reply: *Everything seems to move beyond*
*Our remedy* insomnia but one unhealing wound
yet scans show *acus* relieves a landscape of pain

as Richard forever shifty on the political front
now puts some spin on in the ping-pong game
reduces nuclear threat & where opposed before
normalizes relations makes way for Isaac Stern
for tragic cathartic tanks of Tiananmen Square

as with prescriptive saxes John Adams' music
administers memorial verses to his Pacific tour
with fighter pilots grilled burgers poker & beer
a John the Baptist those "his wilderness years"
adversity his & vatic Tse-tung's finest teacher

relates it generally but mostly to elections lost
painfuller than bodily trauma suffered in war
tells Chou how it wasn't so much his victories
had taught & hardened him but setbacks more
wants from life a single win to surpass defeat

that may have been it even with his Watergate
for as Pat visited another catastrophe or clinic
climbing a quake-ruined wall to commiserate
& Ireland served readers & the afflicted alike
RN crossed opened hurled his doctored strike

# New Gulf

the Sulphur Company's mining town
in an area known as Boling Dome
beside their basic beautiful plant
built to be environmentally sound

in '23 Albert Wolf had scouted the site
without any help from modern geophysics
recommended by him as a promising land
the most he found in the whole Gulf Coast

the unborn composer's dad phoned at Jonah
"there is work if you can be here by tomorrow"
a Depression job & his Model A out of gas
all four of its old tires slick & flat

no clothes or shoes he could show up in
then outfitted at the nearest drygoods store
his car too by the father of a boyhood friend
knew he'd pay it back could always count on him

served on the survey crew for laying it out
laid off then rehired & returned to houses framed
pecans growing along every lettered street
crape myrtles in rows & most dwellings the same

bar ditches seen from screened-in porches
kept clean by the Company & freshly painted
the lawns all mowed & neatly trimmed
though here his mother never quite at home

his father ever with his minor industrial role
its history of locating & smelting sinewy iron
lustrous silver    icy platinum    glittering gold
while this a nonmetal a virile versatile atom

its extremes present in various sulphide ores
at once powerfully vitriolic & strangely docile
elemental sulphur itself "the stone that burns"
this one of free enterprise's brightest stories

from erecting & striking the derricks' rigging
for "discovery of bodies heretofore unsuspected"
embedded in salt caprocks of its coastal hills
removed by Herman Frasch's revolutionary process

of water superheated for melting deepest deposits
pumped up to the surface by their air compressor
to compete with the Sicilian mines' lower costs
as he rose through pipeline ranks to a supervisor

as a driller's helper was where he began
Claude & he both starting at 80 a month
by '57 that buddy at the top as its president
then elected in '68 to be chairman of the board

his dad just as happy among expansion joints
where the gauges & spigots creep back & forth
moved up to miss the fitting & welding of leaks
a craft of not tying down but of letting pipe float

his the joy of Success's thousands at her beck & call
not to be pushed but to follow his leadship's pull
like a geologist with eyes impaired knees from football
out after the unchanging not the confusing & fickle

digging in the earth for its hidden treasure
in contact with its wondrous beauty & power
extracted for a standard of living always higher
any profits depending on a resourceful nature

conserved & reclaimed land stripped & drained
turned a forty-foot dome into a recreational lake
letting cattle graze & slowly the timber revive
renewing pastures until even the buffalo thrive

ran the risk of protracted trials appeals rehearings
a Federal case over lengthy misleading complaints
in court defendants on trading of insiders' shares
their "Perpetual Jeopardy" read by students of law

& from here sent their search around the globe
north through iceberg tips of arctic seas
on a whale boat manned by two Eskimos
to the midnight sun of forbidding reaches

south to Mexico's isthmus of Tehuantepec
unsuspicious Nopalapa between Gulf & Pacific
to the outback Iran Iraq Ethiopia & Egypt
the tantalizing Canadian Shield at Kidd Creek

on the lookout for a clue in that summer swamp
frozen in winter below where dreams can probe
drilling through clay & into rock down 600 feet
in the middle of nowhere gambling against every odd

in a helicopter mounted with electromagnetic detector
checking again on readouts for anomalous zig or zag
by the piles of moose bones ketchup & bottles of gin
to strike a bonanza overlooked by a lonely prospector

through heroic adventures on surveying teams
would measure & map & jockey for claims
then their plane struck a mountain on Baffin Island
the geophysicist one ankle dislocated the other fractured

manages to pull others from out of the wreckage
tending to the pilots both critically injured
for three days when at last all spotted & saved
after eighteen years brought it into production

through each ordeal runs the perseverance theme
by far the strongest point their survival of disaster
then faced disappearance of the Marine Sulphur Queen
a crew of 39 vanishing traceless between Cuba & Keys

that world's first tanker for moving in liquid form
bound with 15,000 tons from Beaumont to Norfolk
the mystery from those dark days remaining unsolved
though by Christmas their sales hit an all-time high

his mother lowest on finding his appetite gone
not eating could ruin his health & threaten his life
then regained it in Wharton at the children's ward
follow-up trips to the pediatrician her only escape

when she ordered her usual at the corner drugstore
a chicken salad sandwich & a fountain limeade
on the drive going & coming her color restored
spirits lifted retelling him of their very first date

then knew they neared home by the sour stench
of mining water running in their drainage ditch
to the son its smokestacks his welcome sign
had arrived at their manicured railroad line

the golf course & club where he first performed
recital pieces shown off before all this town
past the brick post office & along their street
to spot in the sycamore his private treehouse

or to turn to the left & cross over the tracks
could read the disabled report's numbers in red
if none a green light on the bulletin board
by memorial flagpole listing World War dead

from Aguilar to Rodríguez    while those not taken
served the nation by excavating vital brimstone
capping & sealing the wells with mud & cement
his father out in the fields a foreman by then

meeting the prediction it would yield 50 million
after over 70 of long tons "still agoin' strong"
yellow blocks piled first by wood then metal forms
to his dad its 50-foot-high vat a work of art

retained its golden liquid till solidified dry
up on a surface stadium-like but twice the size
its reserve inventory winning in the Axis game
& freedom in raising the ante had upped its price

pushed production & the stocks to record heights
his hardened slab a vision of Coronado's Cities
funded the Houston Symphony for a concert here
through V-Day dividends put its program on the air

constructed the Boy Scouts hut & a reservoir peer
where the son camped & learned to dive & swim
beneath it carved a horse's head on a creosote beam
one of those summers shared with Company friends

among them Nola & Dean & shy Mary López
in overalls & pigtails ever kept her distance
their cabins separated by a big vacant patch
rode his bike there to visit but was not let in

told simply "it's just not done by either side
we have ours & you over there have your own lives
meet on the job    at school    or at the restaurant
where we feed you Anglos jalapeños & enchiladas"

shut down & only cattle egrets now fly or stand
white sentinels among the weeds & rusting pipe
since a French conglomerate took over the plant
the workers either transferred out or told to retire

his house & so many others hauled off or leveled
managers' row half vacated though still superior
like the director's mansion with its stunted palms
its bungalow for foreign dignitary or state governor

nothing much of this missed in his mother's thoughts
happier in Beaumont when they moved from it all
each duplicate street    every predictable shift
Company stores decorated with the same reindeer

wanted for him a bigger a far brighter future
looking back remembered the drawing he'd made
of a keyboard on paper where his fingers played
the phrases he heard & would scribble however

but knew even then he must have the real thing
must study with the only teacher a few blocks away
in their uncertainty would drive him over to Houston
he impatient for delivery when the lessons began

dashed to her house across neighboring yards
scales repeated with her idols all looking down
busts of Mozart Schubert Tchaikovsky & Chopin
loaned him her priceless records & favorite scores

carried him to the opera & introduced the stage
then quickly her technique not up to his own
outgrown though never those gummed gold stars
the reward given by an old maid her piano in view

of the hospital whose expected was a witness to
an elementary watched over & corrected his script
a penmanship would lead to the measureless bars
to notes & ties for a linking of the close & far

a serial composition could explore & convert
as a foreman-father's lines to float & expand
discover a jagged melody in the electronic scan
rise above as smokestack & a mother had urged

his "Cortege for Orchestra" in memory of her
his burden of paying tribute by a 12-tone row
to one lost & mourned in that mysterious Bermuda
no heavier load ever to leave any Texas port

the perpetual risk taken some plaintiff might sue
file for copyright infringement of his minor sixth
misjudge the timbre of which instrument to choose
the peril of notating & transposing of sexual pitch

& yet through harmony & discord coming to prove
how from deepest swamps & most acrid odors
even the smallest place can hope to produce
love's slow procession in triumphal taste

at Kennedy Center performed his "Museum Pieces"
compared in their way with Mussorgsky's *Pictures*
his operatic setting of Chekhov's *Three Sisters*
a recollection of home abandoned of parting kisses

his saxophone quintet & two elegies for flute
rising & falling to feelings' supply & demand
pumping other hearts with emotions heated & cooled
under her influence who taught a pipe-fitter's gang

guided to the Seven of Cíbola by a Mexican's lot
by way of bitter streams to music's Elysian Fields
through soundings of this jerkwater idyllic spot
to empty rooms filled with the unforgettable

## Muleshoe

every town has its tale
known for sandhill crane
this still remembers the most
a storied high school coach
George Washington by name

no Delaware to row across
no snow as at Valley Forge
rarely even a drop of rain
only had his latest football team
couldn't win a single game

the community's spirits lower
the higher the half-time score
the visitors always far ahead
by 50 points or even more
but rehired for his gallows humor

his fabled lockerroom pep talk
delivered for yet another lost cause
Get on back out there boys
dig in & try to save
some of the equipment

Now let us pray

## Liberty Hill

brutally handcuffed & driven
from here to the county seat
by a sheriff's deputy
at illegal speeds

booked & fingerprinted
locked up in a reeking cell
on orders of a one-armed
Justice of the Peace

whose courtroom behind the bench
sports a pair of famous photos
of Judge Roy Bean's
"Law West of the Pecos"

this just 40 miles northwest
of the capital city
home to high tech & legislature
the State's largest university

car impounded & bail set
all because had questioned
his taking of the perjured word
of a daughter's abusive jerk

had jumped the backyard fence
forced the front door open
insulted & threatened since
she said she wouldn't see him again

happened this spring a year ago
now here to attend this dedication
at their International Sculpture Park
didn't have to return for

yet came to honor Fowler's art
RAF pilot San Antonio born
pioneer jet fighter in Korea & 'Nam
earned a Bronze Star & a Purple Heart

in retirement started a new career
hammering out his "Libertarian"
with arm-like branches bent above
& below a faceless patch of

head-shaped stone bears the cross
lifts high a David's star & a torch
all dated bicentennial July Fourth
signed it simply Mel his tabby too

yellow abstract with pyramid ears
called it "Liberty Cat" of course
legs head & tail displaced but there
to be found like freedom's Cheshire

dead in Italy at 69
fell from a ladder & drowned
facedown in a puddle just inches deep
though had by then fulfilled his dream

his private vision to bring
the nations to Precinct No. 2
to catch them in the creative act
as from a single piece his garden grew

his ashes scattered as willed
from a vintage Stearman biplane
among these native oaks & hills
where a figure a year would rise or recline

Jean-Paul Phillipe of France's
"Tirez moi de la"
an actual rope in limestone
a soundless kind of Liberty Bell

from Japan Mihama rolled
twisted the rock as dough
log-sized loaves of bread
baked in time's geologic stove

Tom Piccolo's "Blanca mujer"
her torso a type of cello
with cedar beams bolted where
strings could throb pizzicato

Ann Merck's Western nude
her hair in a Victorian bun
on her stomach with buttocks up
fingers touching to shade the sun

an unsigned limbless creature
with its parts separated into three
on one pink surface carved graffiti
toward whose meaning it seems to crawl

Jim Thomas's "Forgotten Ancestors"
bronze cobwebbed cowskull star-
shaped spur-helmeted conquistador
his eye socket pupil a living spider

others by West German Canadian Pole
but now unveil Melville's masterpiece
when dignitaries pay belated tribute
those never thought he'd ever do it

Land Office reps     a Senator's staffer
Endowments & Commissions lent no aid
officials here today to win swing votes
most like the J.P. named but didn't show

as the ribbon's cut citizens ooh & aah
at the blue-grey veined Italian marble
of Mel Fowler's "Misterio di vita"
posthumous gift for the welcome they gave

to Renata Reck came to sculpt & stayed
to Don Cunningham school administrator
who helped to secure this adjacent tract
for their high school museum out-of-doors

to locals who provided tools of the trade
a place to put up & home-cooked meals
from their unmown lots the raw materials
solid sedimentary & metamorphic support

for the daily constructing & chipping away
all captured & preserved on video
by James Vaughn an ex minor-leaguer
now restores steam engines & diner cars

as even in these smallest of kicker towns
have learned to discover at least two sides
first & lasting impressions
the Jekylls & Hydes

## Laredo

for most it means a place to cross
to enter the exotic or escape the plague
for those who stay the offering's backyard oranges
signs in either language or a Spanglish mix

where *menudo* boils for breakfast
stomach linings instead of *Wheaties*
in the evening over coals the *tripas* dripping
intestines on tortillas red with chilis

while wombs deliver their stash of stuff
pass through customs a hundred grams
others swimming for paycheck dreams
to drown    swelter in fields    or rot in jail

for compared to where they're headed for
this city on the Rio Gran' can hold no candle
though its sun's unsnuffed    seems never to set
only cactus a wax unmelted by that endless wick

& though night descends as torrid as day
yet polkas blaring & the *Coronas* sweating
have provided a paradise on either side
a whore from Jalisco adding something more

or so it seemed before the buzz wore off
& watched her undress in damp adobe
the room cramped by commode & bed
her skinny legs thinned ugly

the bikini panties ringing her feet
the bra falling away from nothing to show
lying there thinner on the soiled pink sheet
covering withered nipples with toilet tissue

till standing embarrassed & ashamed
hardly regretting the loss of manhood or money
hated most to know how true they were
those sophomore stories all ended in impotent pity

though that was then    had still to hear him
for the world is not as some have said
it doesn't stop with a temper tantrum
or languish holed up like a jilted lover

even in sand watermelons will swell
from pig-tail vines to hogshead barrels
their lengthwise shades of two-tone green
quenching the eyes    thirst by an inner oasis

as even now another memory arrives
to bridge a wider border than the river's flood
to bring together more than contentious blood
or settle disputes over how rule & whose system

with Beauty & the kids returned by train
irate at being laid over on Villa's side
by a misunderstanding of schedule & rates
by a travel agent in the efficient States

stuck at the site of that ancient rite
took a leaking room overlooked a squalid plaza
where the same shoeshine boys & *chicle* vendors
went their shabby rounds as if forever

then ate at a *lonchería* where the workers came
clean & reasonably priced    the waitress polite
later paid to ride in a horse-drawn carriage
in among the pasteled walls of tree-lined streets

with currency converted & a mind slowly turning
away from all the visions would prostitute
a wanting to change more than coins or currents
to remake the life of any loathsome place

could suddenly hear the driver speaking
of the houses & homes like a calloused hand
whose history he'd known almost from birth
spoken in Spanish with a pride would understand

## Kountze

self-advertised as
"the town with a
sense of humor"

more famous around
these conservative parts
for Archer Fullingim's

liberal notes
hot coals
in his weekly *News*

but mostly a milestone
one more on the highway home
merely a joke on speeding through

to a Scout or church camp
or a delicious swim
in sandy treacherous

Village Creek
on a hunting trip near
like the one for squirrel

when with the safety off
awaited a shot already knew
would surely miss

no good with a gun
unable even to stomach
the imagined sight of

a bloodied living thing
when dad decided
to smoke him out

to set a small twig fire
at the base of the inverted
v-shaped hole

of that hollow tree
had seen him scamper & take to
till it caught inside

blazed out of control
watched as the flames
leaped limb to limb

suddenly engulfed
that whole
dead trunk

on driving back through
dad saying not to worry
it wouldn't catch the woods

yet thoughts went red & black
filling up with infernal clouds
could see & then could hear

the forest floor ignite
a roar sent up by every acre
& through his decision not to phone

to a ranger lookout station
could picture the charred stumps
of pecan & pine

all now a kind of historical marker
no granite slab with a metal seal
in the State's panhandle shape

bearing that month day & year
but on the map of routes
dirt or paved

of the roads
to love & trust
this memory

smolders yet
would just as soon forget
nothing more's

worth naming here
unless it's maybe
a performance on

their dew-wet football field
when the marching band
took first division

or the date from this country place
whose father ran a filling station
with its clean inspected restrooms

its *Mosinee* towels
its liquid soap a yellow-green
& the key like *Pennzoil*

"asked for"
she a Methodist
wouldn't kiss if implored

sitting long hours at a drive-in screen
through wildly impassioned Hollywood scenes
praying they would rage & spread to her

but that too a fire in a hollow tree
was to burn itself so quickly out
the way all along he said it would

another minor landmark
known only as
good for a laugh

## Johnson City

at the boyhood home
of LBJ
wisteria reaches out
wanders & twines

crape myrtles stand
giraffes in bloom
their splotched
albino skins

stuck with dried
cicada shells
dropping them when
the parchment curls &

falls away
liveoaks with
their lopped-off limbs
delay arthritic bends

the peach    a miniature
bears the heat
so its fruit is left
sun-ripened red

mimosa hackberry
magnolia cedar
all here branching within
an unbarbed fence

inside the house
his forensic text
lying open still
in the living room where

he learned to speak
of how to shed
to outgrow
& yet live on

to save the past in
a city block
then take it deep
as rural light & water

can turn to sweetest sap
to advance    to move on up
to fly worldwide
in Air Force One

to review the troops
the missing in action
loss of arms & legs
to bombs & mines

though not for long
nor ever so far
a Chief-Executive cattleman
can't climb back in

a Hill Country saddle
to ride the coastal bermuda
to a ranch-style brand
of gelding humor

in time for
a Saturday barbecue
for a visit to strength-
renewing settlers' graves

said the best manure
for any land
is its owner's own
familiar step

& though this tall
drawling leader's gone
his grasses still green up
to fatten beeves

& barring a
late spring frost
orchards promise
a record crop

these husbandry leaves
agree or disagree
with a campaign run
at rhetoric's cost

## Jarrell

the town that lost a subdivision
now you see it now you don't
shown far & wide on television
in the wake of twisters spawned

by a whirling boiling funnel
sucked petty complaint & fear
of poor service or unpaid bill
all suddenly lifted to disappear

moans over taxes & electric rates
though those soon enough return
unlike the families lived on streets
with fireplaces & kindling to burn

their plumbing & slabs of cement
walls of wood brick or limestone
whining dogs tied up or fenced
horses cows & tractors gone

scattered by a slaughtering air
their rodeo arena & trailer park
swept away as if were never there
picked for the dance by a dark

swaying partner carried them off
fast-forwarding beyond the pale
into the everlasting arms of soft
savage clouds left survivors wail-

ing some losing others to renew
their childhood faith in a greater
plan a higher will no camera crew
close-up can ever hope to capture

the newpapers' front-page spread
stirred urgent calls from Tennessee
with a supermarket gutted & 30 dead
from far away as Chile phoning to see

all were safe from a jumbled sequence
friends checking in with a sigh of relief
viewed the footage of shocking events
called into question each trust & belief

though outpouring donations & aid
from neighboring towns & cities
have recalled how Marshall made
Europe join in refitting industries

rebuilding after a devastating war
as here even missing houses & kin
pets caught in a pathway of horror
tornado alley or no they begin again

## Houston

the air was heavy with wet
heavier on a bright muggy day
when mosquitoes floated
out of the bayou mouths
in thick humming breaths
swarming so you would nearly choke
or if not    then gag on chemical clouds
of the fumigator's nightly spray

it was a weather stuck with you
more than men    everything
was close    clothes in summer
sucking the sweat    gray sky kissing
the morning mist    closets of damp & mildew
apartments compact as hives
though honeyless    everything close    except the lives
those    more often asunder

a stadium of voices from every state
urgent accents from East & West
a U. of Michigan graduate
once linebacker on a Rose Bowl team
turned a 9-to-5er in a bruising Bank & Trust
or the man Prudential Insurance moved
with wife & kids    from their Connecticut dream
reshowing the Hartford slides hoping it somehow soothed

come to a complex from the country    the only Texans there
that pup    a few months old    blown apart
by the dogcatcher's high-powered legal weapon
the church bazaar & cakewalk
on an asphalt court of St. Vincent de Paul
when allowance went for naught
the junior high dance when would never dare
hold her near    all the days it wasn't fun

rules seemed so hard to learn
multiplication tables bored
swimming nude made the cheeks burn
in games only the bullies scored
& then    any lessons were lost on weekends
when nothing made so much sense
as trading the kid with a Mohawk strip for Batman comicbooks
or watching on that first TV "Boston Blackie" catching crooks

in nearby woods each knew how red & black
was a friend of Jack
how red & yellow
could kill a fellow
yet on the streets or in the halls
could never quite distinguish
all    red black or white    seemed corals
cold snakes of injustice

even knowing the names of trees
memorizing dates    *i*s before or after *e*s
made nothing right or easier
the girl with rheumatic fever
who could never leave her room
only the half-wit spoke with her
mashing his nose against the screen
once recovered she found him a bother

but enough of this
every ledger has another side
& on it one can list
those have made it a matter of pride
to have spent eight months in this metropolis    though known
more for NASA & the artificial turf of the Astrodome
than for those converted to countless gain
their long nights of loneliness & pain

think of Bracker that longtime friend
who wrote of life with his father here
in a simple four-line poem that pays
true homage to the man & his tender ways

recall how Vassar Miller's sonnets mend
a broken spirit    taking care
the boney wisdom    the metered touch    offset
a body born in the red

hear Stokowski & the symphony orchestra
heaping the city's treasure store
with an Ives or a Villa-Lobos score
& after Barbara Jordan's puissant speech    hurrah!
for the election gave her a seat    more for the vote she cast
to bring men closer than a coastal climate
enter them all as accounts receivable    a balancing of hate
a summing in solvent black what once appeared but a bankrupt past

# Honey Island

not far from Sour Lake
it never is
for in this State as anywhere

the same farm road
can always lead
from sweet to bitter    bitter to sweet

those early settlers stuck such names
on these Texas towns & cities
though in each the memories & meanings change

since just as one will envision at times
an inviting isle    an Atlantis jewel
in a stagnant pond of a setting

so in the one the other may dwell
a transmuting of land or water
depending most on who was there

& if she went along
to boat or swim
or stole away with another

sneaking off to skinny dip
or paddled out with him
to an Eden there in the grass

left behind on the green-scummed shore
or given such looks sent one rowing alone
to that mired mosquito grove

as when the class took its senior trip
to a picnic beside these double pools
where the girls let down their hair

showed more than cheerleaders doing splits
at pep-rallies forming a pyramid tip
while here jocks bared their chests

dangling from a high-dive board
in chinning to flex
their bronzed biceps

& would covet all they had
their perfect flips & jack-knives
their lovely breast & butterfly strokes

yet dreamed of something more
knew even then could never sport
brains to match their brawn or beauty

only feelings forever feared to show
a hopeless love that surely stood
as clearly out as all their parts

bulging in tight bikini trunks
or shapely in strapless bathing suits
till time has slowly conceived a line

not one intends to impress
the way they won their hottest dates
but one to record & return that day

for this go-round by reading aright
the highway sign to its Thicket knoll
am getting & having it over & over

as here above the towering pines
have stopped the sun
to let it shine

off emeralds liquified
off ambered skins aglow
with a tan will still survive

long winters after the last of those
believing their lives spent & over
have lost all sight of this paradise

now to bring it back tenfold
by this word-hoard recompense
with its pleasure-pained recall

# Hebbronville

## 1. a sonnet of prospects

had no idea where in creation you were
just a beginning position as English teacher
unprepared for the learning ahead
of a love of wastes & their Mexican blood
though at first sight no    more then of relief
after crossing a hundred miles of sand & mesquite
driven to you through Beeville Benavides Realitos
what royalities? what realities? what silver roads?
when nothing grew but scenery progressively worse
its paintless shacks & desolate sun-baked tracts
all clear signs of exile into a small-town hell
then sighted your domed Franciscan church
its turquoise visible atop that relative hill
its promise of vision from the barrenest facts


## 2. a teenage novelette

walking to school would sink in the sand
as a hot gusting wind covered the tracks
in August sun a wool the one decent suit

her first day too in that brand-new building
its inlaid blue rotunda only halfway done
its tiles & the long grammar lessons still to come

kept her overcoat on & buttoned in class
asked to borrow a copy of Austen or Brontë
her round tan face her soft brown eyes

then the father expelled    all-district ball-handler
made a handsome pair he beside her tall & thin
intended for more each year than babies & beans

a modern facility erected with taxes on oil & gas
an outpost of education dropped in semi-desert
at the perimeter its parasite plants like invaders in wait

she couldn't   was gone by October never to return
took the books to her home   was met at the screen
said she didn't care to read anymore

before blackboards could fill with triangles & squares
the halls cleared of drifting dunes & diamond rattlers
their encroaching attacks held off at what high cost

standing guard one night at the football stadium
watched as students stoned another coiling snake
heard its warning music slow to a fading phone call

a poisonous viper with the markings of higher math
though its venom no match for lines drawn by color
deadly mouth sounds imitating saxon & conquistador

did he ever shoot another ten-foot jumper
might free throws sunk have gained racial ties
or did cacti root again instead of fans


3. initiation theme

was invited to join the club
"Cardinal Puff" where it's chug-a-lug
on missing each time any ritual move

the Spanish speakers treating the two newcomers
the other a junior high art instructor name of Jacks
all the rest were teaching in senior grades

he coming on strong trying to fit right in
acted as if he could even be a Mexican's friend
but lost the test   his talk didn't last long either

valued their company more than winning that game
yet in celebrating hadn't noticed them switch
his boilermaker they had earlier mixed

driven home by Popo & gotten into the shower
to fall asleep standing leaning in that running water
collapsed in bed sick for weeks from the slightest smell

that roommate mocking & saying what a silly *gringo*
then taught a rhyme all in *español*
of *tuna luna laguna* can still recall


4. a farewell note

cleft in two on that final day
happy to go sorry not to stay
then found on the amplifier
a white chicken feather

left there without any hint
as to what it meant
unless it somehow said
have felt too often afraid

of whom or of what
they hadn't bothered to jot
on or in the envelope
thought it was maybe a joke

though no mystery was there
have known too much of fear
will always expect the worst
worry even on coming in first

so certain wherever may land
is the place they forever damn
to the most unbearable weather
those worthy so much better

then meet the Saenz twins
*latino* students with toothy grins
who after their geometry class
work at pumping regular gas

small goofy & eager guys
with bright farsighted eyes
average grades & college hopes
who surprise by showing the ropes

helping even to overcome
the thinking one clum-
sy puny pitiful & slight
can still stand up & fight

how the one who's afraid
is the one who's made
what any feather's meant
the message never sent

# Fort Worth

## I. Cowtown

the place of birth
the only kind of earth
this    loose & dry    mixed with red
hackberries    shale broken but unrusted as toy regiments of lead
forged from melted type & toothpaste tubes    a man can ever seem
to understand    whose every shrub gives off a dream
of all he meant to be
the purple bloom pungent scent exotic leaf of the Vitex tree
meshed in the mind with a heroic view
to that other self the fading one one knew
to climb limbs & like a sniper sheltered there
swear eternal truth to something somewhere
sensed again perhaps if one could but return
to soil & bark the same than coming rather to learn
the house is gone the aroma of ardor long chopped down
a city block of decisive victories lost to an unknown town

yet even then there survive the atmosphere
enough of the sounds & smells year after year
to tell how the simplest thing
may in the end mean everything
the Indian arrow in late September
from a weed whose name one can't remember
three inches long or so    pulled from the plant
a living quiver    wetted with tongue & lips to slant
the feathery barbs & make them stick
in a schoolmate's cotton polo shirt    prick
him into an excited yell
an exchange of harmless darts before the final bell
for this one thanks the limits have proved an endless source
a needed perennial force
that even in its altered way
feeds one still on fields & flowers of a green & referent day

## II. Crawfishing

surrounded by a shopping center now
Black Bridge is where would always go
when just the name was mystery enough
the eeriest atmosphere in all Fort Worth
what with its fields of stunted post oak
would cross three sets of railroad tracks
the first saw in the second war trains
park awhile troops throw candy rations
to neighborhood kids who barefooted
well-supplied with bacon strips & white
string would green-stain soles on summer's
grass dropping lines down holes to tease
them out & though war's sweet no more
feet grown sore from waiting for a sale
still nothing's acquired without a catch
the old trestle replaced by a brand-new
parking lot its pale blue moons the bait


## III. Grade School

1st

George C. Clark
a red brick elementary
with fenced & asphalt playgrounds
cement drinking fountains    Dick & Jane

the man was named for never known
ever confused him with
that patriot & pioneer
another revolutionary died in rags

who marched his same 200 men
back & forth before a British fort
like beginnings at this one-time army post
trooping them out again

to trick the past into surrendering
to trace where it all began
not where any dream went wrong
but why the poem persists

yet where to go from here
with rhythm & rhyme in full retreat
the garrison of verse now under attack
by a swamp-infested guerrilla force

no set form a copter can spot
at times a clearing in any wood
or a 6 year-old with a handgrenade
strapped to his one good leg


2nd

Miss Harvey
of the heavy wooden desks
seats shaped to skinny cheeks
up one flight    2nd grade on the 2nd floor

a rising bodily to new heights new horizons
the promising lessons she gave
of miraculous letters read & written
but where did she go at the end of day

in her dark print dresses
always wine or navy blue
her sagging face
of an ashen cast

long window shades lowered for naps
heads down on the hard ink-welled tops
sums & subtractions copied from boards
whose mystic keys would never let in

to that room where no sun came
where the black cat curled
on velvet & sequined sofa
asbestos logs fired by the cold gas jet

as she rocked & marked the pages torn
from the *Big Chief* tablets
dreaming on the doctors & lawyers
the PhDs her laboring would bear

on the poet would deliver
her cinderella soul
from that stepmother & her fat-footed daughters
night    insomnia    regret


3rd

up Hemphill Street
not quite to Fina's
Tortilla Factory
sycamores lining the way
from O.L.V.
those initials standing for
Our Lady of Victory
the parochial school
black & white & castle-like
among the resined cedars
so spooky beneath the moon

on weekdays pedaled by
to the public attended free
with nickels to spend
where a screendoor wore
its "Dad's Ol' Fashioned"
rootbeer sign
whose phrase said fast
came out "dazzlefashin"
the store supplied a wondrous yo-yo
buy one there & see it carved
with palm trees seemed to sway
notched by a real live Filipino
"rocked the cradle"
"walked the dog"
took one "round the world"

to win a Columbia bike
would save those filler coupons
though never won
dad had to buy it instead
the one with longhorn handle bars
bent against an unseen car
whose driver stopped in time
the lie told when was showing off
for the Catholic girls
in their cute Scotch plaids
with matching satchels
the math & grammar still going on
somehow before & after
those trips both morning & noon
to that grocery across the street
its candied world
of grab bag & licorice jar

never far from
memory's reach
its performance
as with a string
tied from middle or index finger
to a round exotic wood
can spin & return
now to then
all the lessons
still to learn

4th

introduction to Spanish
another language
& love
the same

her notes passed
when reason the teacher
turns her head
an approximation

but close
as any can come
the accent ever
giving away

not native to
the land where
flowers blossom
out-of-season

where birds
sing with-
out expecting
spring to stay

        *   *   *

as pitcher at recess
felt handsome & fit
with all the right stuff
the team on which
was just beginning
to belong left behind
Susy who saved a place
a seat just next to hers
in the dining hall
but most of all
that mole by lips
of a face whose name

got lost in the move
her smooth olive cheeks
unkissed in the cloak-room
not even off-stage
waiting in the wings

from the mimeographed program
of those forever have had a part
hers the leading role
in that primary play
or was it more the recognition scene
fear of an end to the act

first love in storage
reclaimed at last
& in memory's care
not so damaged as packed
in a Van Lines crate

María saying was rather
some special handling for her
but way before her spring
before could even guess
a cedar from the star's routine
there had to be
the transfer in winter
to that long low building
that off-white brick
stained russet by the wind-blown sand

the one-story like a continuous first grade
no more graduating to an upper floor's view
sitting apart then at the back of the room
a know-it-all believing
there was nothing new
picking up habits still haven't dropped
like holding this pen
with a thumb in the air
or worse even
with the nose up there

for even back then
had it even been known
would have surely declared
had made that Trail of Tears
in a five-hour drive

a short trip north
to the Red River where
its south fork
marked off more
than Longhorn from Sooner

into Oklahoma    eyewitness report
as if it had been in fact part of a plan
seeing now how would come to watch
daddy grow into a man
battling alone far from his kin
with bankers & insurance men

selling farmers up to his cuffs in ruddy mud
their irrigating tubes flooding the fields
of wheat cotton alfalfa & sorghum
or in that cellar smelled of rotten spuds
huddled as a tornado
ripped through the gin

& the unattractive Michigan girl
unattractive as she
two strangers ahead of the class
that gray afternoon would take her home
back to the barracks
of the air force base at Altus
abandoned in postwar days
her father in braces hobbled to the car
his muscled arms & calloused hands
his thin misshapen legs
nothing for a boy but to dream of the past
nothing of beauty in all that land

& though for years it offered no fruit
was yet the setting where this writing took root
& tasteless & green as it keeps coming out
have that red earth to thank if what it's about
is salt
instead of theatrics


## IV. Mary Frances Keetch (1890-1976)

### 1. A Guided Tour of Granny's Yard

pardon me hon' I'll have my
breath just here in a jiffy
this old lawnmower wears me
near to a nub    got to where
she's cranky as they swear I
am    bogs down so

till this grass will be
the death of me
now don't you fret yourself one bit
you just come on over here
them there? why them's dwarf larkspur
reddens next to 'em is poppies

my son's only daughter
Betty Boop I always call her
she's the one wanted them planted
the spring it was
I'd brung her back to visit
from Oklahoma City    her very

first trip on a train    she stayed on here
couldn't say how long    a month for sure
they none of them comes anymore
this messy mimosa's 'bout done for
onct it dies I won't put up with anothern
drops these brown blooms like

dirty drawers all over the goldfish pond
bad as having males about the house
had roomers here in the war    sailors
worked at the Navy Hospital's psychiatric
ward    put a straightjacket on me at a party
that oak?    squirrels have a nest high up in

this old hackberry    I s'pose they's the ones
hid the acorn    yes I'm crazy
'bout rocks too    Doodie Bug my younger
daughter's older boy he picked
this one up down at the corner lot
said he'd brain me with it

if my bird friends
didn't stop telling me
every wrong thing he'd start to do
I used to catch him
before he could break the limbs
climbing in this Vitex tree

he always thought they flew
to that redwood feeder and talked to me
I did to them    still do    but they . . .
rushing off so soon? well honey come back by
anytime    I'm always here    just yell
that door bell ain't worked in years


2. Granny's Fruitcake

some said she was nutty as one
stayed out in the summer sun
to weed or gather lilies & moss
from her double goldfish pond
so long it cooked her addled brains
furrowed skin on her weathered face
browned like delicious sugary crusts
descended from a bunch of Crackers
fled Rome where during Sherman's
scorching march hid smoked hams

from damned Yankees right beneath
her Ma who did her deathbed scene
moved to Alba named some thought
for the oldest Latin town or salt deposits
just beyond mainly meant to make it clear
no blacks allowed "Boy, don't you dare
get off that train" hard brazil nuts she
would soften to "'igger toes" chopped in
with broken pecans candied cherries pine-
apples sliced green citron her heavy batter
mixed in a surplus Plexiglas navigator dome
from the Convair bomber plant weighed &
baked two thousand pounds in tin pans rec-
tangular or round cooled then wrapped in
wine-soaked rags in waxed paper decorated
with cypress sprigs & cedar cuttings from her
award-winning yard she mowed & trimmed
kept it herself selling cakes to companies as
Christmas gifts eaten all those carefree days
never once conceiving such a checkered past
could make them taste so good


V. Sis & Alvin's Bathroom

for years would come here
on business & pleasure
to the source of all words
they never used once
& if any mouth would dare to
she washed it out with soap & water

where to latch both doors
kept unzipped cousins
from being caught by the pigtailed sort
or taken by surprise as naked as jays
kept the other from knowing
that secret difference    thrilling as ever
a glorious enigma still to this day
though let in on it by a wedding in Chile
by love & the birth of a son & daughter

to open them both inwards revealed
the scenes & senses have sought to return
released through either to run circling around
from the bedroom in front to a favorite in back
sharing there the popped black kernels
hearing The Fat Man    Inner Sanctum    The Shadow
long before an end to the war-&-peace decades
those chapters of their fixing it up    & now that it is
it still isn't really    at least not looking from here

where out this uncurtained window
the cottonwood seeds an early snow    its trunk
big around as a barrel    only cut down later
& hauled away    when a dead limb damaged
their roof    its insides hollowed & polished smooth
by woodpeckers living & eating within
through unconscious summers    while
the two of them worked on it little by little
as on memory it has forever since

the oval mirror still hung in the attic
awaiting to be set in its antique frame
to give not these but their dreamed-of reflections
above the widened & tiled washbasin
would replace the old was rusted & chipped
crowded about for scrubbing combing brushing
for loading of pistols & shooting through screens
to power a boat by candle or a wound rubberband
for stocking of tadpoles crawdads or goldfish

before the linoleum got ripped up for good
its pattern of dots & colored designs
grew faded & marked with mysterious shapes
worn from scuffing or splashing the floor
from dashing in & out & back & forth
when both would yell "don't bang that door"
its covering become a galaxy or atlas of maps
with planets or countries all named & peopled
by creatures never discovered in any elementary reader

the wallpaper had known a far better day
but never to visiting nieces & nephews
who made out in stains the brown-edged faces
friendly at noon    so frightening by night
in spots bare timber & nail heads showed through
bathing feet at bedtime how often would squint
to decipher the signals & the messages sent
disguised by masks of gauze-like webbing
kept ever uncertain kept forever guessing

the doubled lip of the white iron tub
retold its age    that its hour had come
though filled with youth    with coffers & ships
to a spilling over from that plunging below
for treasures sunk to its murky bottom
while it dripped its last as ticks on a clock
& yet by the unmatching handles of spigots
the broken for cold    the enameled for hot
still answered with a liquid of timeless relief

the new commode would have no brick
at rest in its sweat-lined tank    the reason unclear
perhaps for raising water to the cut-off quicker
to float its bulb like a big coppered bud
would stopper an insistence ran on & on
a tune the adults couldn't stand to hear
its song to them such a monotonous whine
but with a heaviness like that at its heart
how could it ever have hoped to flower

was reassured by the cleansing aroma
of linen dried in Tuesday light    if cloudy
inside on a collapsable rack    patched folded stacked
in closets would never shut tight    leaked a freshness
of towels laundered in their kitchen washer
pulled through its handcranked wringer
rubbed on a tin-rippled board
blued from a bottle    on its red & black label
a funny prim matron    her hair in a bun

now shiver to glance at the ivy outside
darkens the ground with its hole-pocked slabs
paving a walk between these houses & yards
granny's across the way     its chimney & shrubs
its unlit living & dining where she wandered alone
cursing grandaddy who at last had up & left her
could endure no more of Nan's nagging complaints
drove to Meridian Mississippi where a widow woman
would watch with him his loved minor league

he'd built their house without letting Nan know
copied from one like it in Dallas she so despised
from its site downtown moved it here next door
"plum outa town & nearly in the country"
the maid would grumble   worked on awhile for granny
he selling this one to his stepdaughter & his son-in-law
who that year of Wall Street's fall first made it home
their fiftieth now recalling all the families reared
uplifting histories would hear winter to autumn

not of a Machine Gun Kelly holed up in Fort Worth
who took his first sub out of a local pawn
robber & kidnapper still unwanted dead or alive
but in '33 of their gardening & mowing the lawn
holding up through wetters of wallpaper & beds
the breaking of fixtures & forgetting to jiggle
their footing the bills for fuel & freezers of cream
for cooling off in August from a hundred degrees
as they saved & planned to remodel one day

to most their city means only a radio show
with Bob Wills & the Doughboys fiddling to sell
Light Crust flour & Pappy's gubernatorial bid
yet for some that music has never soaked in
only such sights & sounds as come from this
the unmentionable room     its unspeakable poem

VI. The Stockyards

the place of death
where the bright free age of grazing grass
where the trails & rails led & it came to pass
a hammer's blow snuffed their need for breath

is a half-suspected self
avoided as that avenue at night
known as "cut & shoot"    where winos rent at the famed Right
a hotel roomed ranchers    now but those who are on the shelf

of the many have gone & left
of those too born here or raised
in search of art or peace have pulled up stakes
stand here alone now strangely bereft

to stare at where the packinghouse shell
looms cold & burnt    its panes all cracked
with ladders scaling roofless walls    smokeless stacks
alone to account or make up for a kind of hell

could not be faced    like General Meade
chasing Mexicans to make them take it back    Texas    Hades
others escaping this "culture gulch" by heading East
to write off what gave roots as just bad seed

like those acknowledging little or none
of what went on    knew it more as myth
than any way of life willed or lived with
all the while having steak    eating t-bone

till on this ninety-degree day now overlook
two branches of the Trinity River
from bluffs watch Clear & West forks gather
where the Comanche camped    took

his time    pitching his symboled tent
unperturbed by tornadoes drifting around
thought nothing would ever let them touch down
not here    a sacred spot    taken over since by the Power Plant

now driving down the viaduct
descend to what was once a ritzy section
given over since to Boys Clubs    Golden Gloves    Mexican
food-to-go    come next to the Livestock

Exchange    a sand-colored structure
still a stop for cattle buyers    its style
of Arabic arches & red Spanish tile
housing sellers of sheep & hogs    a poster picture

of a champion steer    & out the back
its steps caked with half-digested hay
raked off handmade boots    lead to charolais
short horn    white face    black

angus    an auction arena    an amphitheatre
with its ribbed silver-painted fence
a half octagon holding ephemeral prints
of hooves destined to patch the dinnerware

with their mucus-colored glue
the dirt on the stage-like floor trampled powder soft
the performance attended by rows & rows of off-
white straws    hats stained by rain & sweat    not a shoe

on any foot    the show beginning when the electric doors
swing to welcome them in    bunches of half-grown cows
frightened as amateur actors    announced to the house
by the auctioneer singing a song of trills & figures

"Gi' me a half gi' me
got 24 gi' me a quarter
25 need a quarter
29.75 now 3"

two men with long smooth sticks
herd the group    hitting it hard
till bidding's done    when exits part
close on rears    receiving fearful kicks

outside among the pens whips crack
driving them in    long trucks backed up
to loading chutes    cattle cars coup-
led beside the branding lots    then the pack-

ing house    its name in red & white
though SWIFT has faded    crumbled down to *ift*
a mass of wires & rods    twist-
ed doubled rusted pipe

reaching into rubble    the fire-
ravaged brick as if bombed out
though granted no atom has fallen    no Kraut
or Jap has returned the favor to Convair

today General Dynamics    whose B-24s in squadron
sprouted engulfing clouds    here first spreading wings
to fly not with grains but deadly droppings
while up this wooden ramp longhorns waited in line

moved slowly to the slaughter    the fire an "accident"
burned for months in consuming the blood & fat
a seeping down would soak the wood    the mat-
ted hides    the conflagration hardly making a dent

in the years of calf eyes crushed to bleed
sadly bright on flaying floors    the nightly flames
razing the ruins    emblazoning brands    oily brains
swollen tongues sputtering until all must heed

the meaning of this chapter    this hidden life
the one none has ever cared or dared come upon
not old-fashioned    written by a time gone
by    but that each finds his fingers fit the knife

fashioned this sloping passage spared by tribal spirits
rising still to a gutted    a caved-in corporation
remembrance of even a risen sun's
decline    kinetics the seeming-innocent drive inherits

in reconciling past & present a ramp
for rendering down to what have been & are
ascending higher than a bigger spread    a grand Lone Star
setting instead on less its ancient sanctioning stamp

## Denton

like every other place
is Janus-faced
take its dreamed of campus Kenton blessed
near where an only brother bled to death
on his final trip from picking up a remaining group
of Green Beret reservists the last to parachute

delivered them safely then flipped his truck
on a narrow curve    his stomach crushed
between the driver's seat & the steering wheel
have grieved for years with that lonely feel
of his young life slipping away
three months after graduation two weeks before his
          wedding day

talked Aunt Sis into taking a pilgrimage to its
          hallowed sounds
in summer heat to its celebrated tree-cooled grounds
a home to festivals a division of Columbia Records pressed
a where to buy this treasured album has stood the test
though so scratchy & filled with cuts by imitative combos
a true aficionado would not confess he even knows

much less still listens to this Euel Box Quintet
on "Toddlin'" or "Woodchoppers Ball"    the only regret
never to have caught them in live performance
here in this town for that final chance
for afterwards the valve-trombonist-leader would graduate
see his sax & trumpet his bass & drums all go their separate

ways to public schools where jazz is seldom heard
to some a discouraging word
few on the road with a Herman or Stan a record date with those

neither first nor last chair with East or West Coast studios
can only hope wherever they went
each made music on his chosen instrument

their talents might have been or maybe not
the equal of a fellow alum's like Giuffre whom none forgot
from here Jimmy had gone to join those idols' bands
to star with Shorty Rogers on Atlantic's *Martians*
*Come Back*    his name mentioned on liner notes
with the likes of a Mingus    his tune set off in quotes

his famous "Four Brothers"    left now with not even one
on the outskirts forever of marriage & the job he'd won
never to share with his bride-
to-be a game of golf at the Country Club laid out beside
the Trinity River    to practice on his trap set for another gig
as drummer to roughnecks off an oilfield rig

# Dayton

back before the Peace Corps knew violation
a picker-upper for the end of an insurance day
to listen sober him up & get him safely home

whose heart attack soon after brought disarray
wouldn't go along even if financially helped
of trusting friends & relatives invested savings

dad resigned lost everything was never himself
a bartender's concoction bottled by Canada Dry
to rice growers & cattlemen along the Gulf

but wanted his own corporation for selling Life
to know & be known ran for & elected mayor
only the loss of visits here or to Liberty nearby

according to dad invented the rotation of tires
steering under Spanish moss hung from trees
raised needed capital through a sale of shares

the fun of riding around in that open-air jeep
to write cash-value policies could use for loans
hired as his confidante & his faithful veep

dad did & believed in his boss's big plans
this a fellow had been a fleet-truck mechanic
regretted nothing of this could not understand

of the agent's son in a company daddy forsook
had he stayed on might have rescued the firm
discovered he'd manipulated its common stock

like dad first sold for Great American Reserve
a '50s plenty let any teen soup his Chevy six
a born salesman an organizer but down to earth

picking up & showing off for the local chicks
when Ike spent the long days driving the links
his name the same as that popular beverage mix

of lime sugar & carbonation for adding to gin
a genius dad considered & declared him to be
homebase to Production National's president

# Dallas

encircled by freeway loops
has wished itself a Roman arena
but styled more after Texas Stadium
where gladiators    this time
Christians from Abilene or SMU
take on Lions Bears Rams
while the lawyer-merchant class
spies down night & day
from box seats or tinted glass
spots the animals in goal-line stands
or last ditches along skidrow
below
            too are those looking for his-
tory    staring at tobacco stains on
Federal Building walks    visitors in from Boston
wondering
Is this where our hero bled?
buying his souvenirs    windows Xed
in snapshots where Oswald took his aim
his bullet granting one more wish

such carpet rides lift powerlines
overpasses skyscrapers high
rises hopes of masses    recall
how they were raised for
days    driving here as a family when fall
trips to the State Fair were long & hard
where at last in Sears would try
the cowboy boots had wanted so    like Gene's
or Roy's    but with narrow feet
dad said no    they didn't fit
nothing in Dallas ever does
it's Texas but then it's not
it isn't the West it never was
would have it moved to an eastern spot

partly this comes out as
the talk of a Cowtown boy    Fort Worth-Dallas
called twin cities yet rivals from the start
the real Texas    with cattle & horses
rodeos at Will Rogers Coliseum    versus
the Airport

typical of towns grown near    the closest father & son
are born to carry a rivalry on
Darío's red head sticks
out in any crowd
can be a pain    yet will claim him any time
like all of Texas    or so would rhyme

Big D's a sore thumb too
though giving credit where credit's due
both share winning points
this city can boast of parks & lakes
are a blue-green sketch
for him to sit & draw    match
with watercolor or tempera paints
outdo this description    make a papa proud

carry him back to creeks shaded
by pecan & peach    running clear & cold
over smooth & green-furred rocks    fresh
by willows    in summer a cool conversing    traded
for memos typed at the Apparel Mart    to baskets sold
beside the bridge    their priceless wrinkled pits
brown-black nuts fallen at feet once bared to rip-
ples    rainbow perch    a movement Darío can better catch

need for that his art    need his love
needed Love Field too    a where to land
& seek for him athletic fun    a high-
er flight than had on fleetest jets    a swim-
ming hole for deeper dives than
dips on tollway drives    a where to buy
western boots for the skinny kid
right for walking streets can still recov-

er that magic word will trim shed blood
like a genii whisped
back inside an olym-
pic lamp overrubbed

# Castroville

taking Interstate 35
Onderdonk's bluebonnets still in bloom
skirt the Alamo City on loop
410 an easy air-conditioned drive

> to where in '66 Mother St. Andrew arrived
> three shipwrecks in all she alone survived
> those first sisters setting sail in '63
> long before access road or superhighway

> Father Dubuis who burned with zeal
> brought them over on the *St. Geneviève*
> up the coast through hunger & exposure
> by bogs & swollen rivers past Civil War

> holding through heavy rain their violins
> for bringing song to these barren plains
> against dread scarlet or typhoid fever
> monstrance chalice & statues of saints

> the closest rail connection La Coste
> five miles away & at floodtime marooned
> where its tacky restored train station
> features today a sauna & swimming pool

then going west on 90
all the way from Austin not a single stop
till this light here at Landmark Inn
the Parks & Wildlife running it now

> racked by Lipan & Comanche raids
> their poisoned arrows ended in hooks
> were not to be pulled from any victim
> even more her Bishop's ambitious barbs

treated worse than any slave or convict
after eviction from a house her own sweat raised
nowhere to go none to give her refuge
nor was her life her own to take

blamed for her brother Father Feltin's arrest
each night of exile for those twenty years
wetting her pillow with tears of remorse
underwent surgery with nothing for pain

in part to repay others for the sorrow she'd brought
a blessed sacrifice made in her guiltless state
then at last in the sisters' cemetery laid to rest
at the foot of the mountain still known as Cross

came the time before in December
return now in April to number 8
this room a favorite with newlyweds
in 1940 termed a smokehouse

a one-storey before shots fired at Sumter
later the upper added as a bathhouse
tradition says the only spot to bathe
between San Antonio & Eagle Pass

out this open door
once a window
the pecans' new green
framed as if a picture

one of Rowena Vance's primitive scenes
Vermont schoolmarm painted the Inn
her husband John's hotel circa '57
put his name in above its entrance

with to the left a picket fence
in the foreground a chicken or two
from the back a girl in pinafore
alongside what is maybe a dog

bushy trees swayed by
an invisible breeze
something perhaps a tie-rail
for the traveler's horse

through wire mesh the branches' shadows
dapple with sunlight a distant roof
of the Haass-Quintle gristmill
rippled with rust

between here & its limestone walls
white rails of the painted porch
with against them the black
squares of this patterned screen

    her correspondence & records destroyed
    when Bishop Neraz knifed the pages
    crumpled & lit them all in a wire burner
    itself a reflection of his beaming face

    as flames licked the edges
    blackened their leaves to ash
    her score of years consumed
    two decades of success heartache failure

    upholding the rule of enclosure
    keeping cattle out of the grapes
    her dowry spent for teaching French
    for burning of learning's midnight oil

    deposed for saying just what she meant
    for accusing clergy of seeking diversion
    not trusting recreation with lonely priests
    would drive their foundress out in disgrace

    an excuse for separating the Order from
    its congregation back in Alsace
    to make Divine Providence a Texas branch
    diocesan with the final word up to Neraz

she the first to travel afar
had followed in Father Moye's steps
he in China doing missionary work
seized & dragged into a mandarin's court

his vestments trampled & torn
set afire by decree though all along he believed
they had secretly kept them had known their worth
he lying like Peter when he denied a Bible he hid

a whole history focused upon
this screen door in early spring
viewed from an old four-poster
beneath this ceiling a cistern before

pentagonal first & lined with lead
then peeled & melted down by Rebs
bullets molded for invading Yanks
to rout them or leave them dead

filled from the river by hydraulic pump
big enough for three to bathe at once
heated by a fireplace on the floor below
now lie here so grateful she never did

who planned to when she attended retreats
following then her mentor Padre Pedro
precious needlework ner nanny had learned
she herself taken in by this order in Temuco

who took María to mass the month of Mary
buying for her some sprigs of baby's breath
to carry through incense & up to the altar
Beauty not wanting to miss not a single day

like Sister Arsene who to accompany Mother
had to leave her rosary & her ring behind
Beauty giving up the veil & her beloved Chile
for poverty & primeval solitude of a Texas kind

can see her observing the postulant's rules
silence in dormitories     no talk at table
darkened halls & dusky basements & maybe
homesick & despondent as Sister Clemence

could not adjust to the language & life
set out on foot for Danville 8 miles' distance
in the woods between New Braunfels & Solms
they found her habit intact but only on bones

not alone the triple scourge these sisters endured
of Indian deprivations     cholera     drought
Mother St. Andrew deprived even of holy communion
for being the Bishop said disobedient

Beauty untrammeled & of her own free will
never to kneel at his pontifical throne
though wonder yet if she regrets it still
the not putting on chastity's perpetual robes

envious as the devil to envision her there
her lovely head bared & bowed to his fingers
purified for lifting a strand of her hair
for the investiture had forbidden forever

then led to the room & clothed for him
as the choir by candlelight chants *Te Deum*
after the ceremony as sign of new dignity assumed
to receive flower wreath & his caress of peace

jealous even knowing of their crying need
for such virgin brides to comfort & teach
to practice their frugal unworldly ways
wanting always & ever to have her alone

for a view to where they built their mill
gave their village an industrial mien
so natural the passerby cannot conceive
is in Texas on Henri's farming grant

made their camp under this still dormant pecan
near Apache hunting grounds & dinosaur tracks
where smooth-faced pulleys cast-iron gear shafts
sent water by tunnel to grind the corn & cotton

Jewish-Portuguese-Frenchman allowed who owed
to repay him working on their church & school
while longing for the Rhine & their city of bells
where the azure pottery adorned Alsatian stalls

begrudge them her even knowing their then & now
having to share this bed with how many nuptials
as the Medina swirls in among its cypress knees
reach to hers locks unravished by religious vows

## Burnet

dad had driven here to have an excuse
for those born & raised there is no choice
though given one later many will choose

never to leave even such a godforsaken place
since wherever it is is where the memories are made
stay on for any through whatever loss

each season the scoring run or pass replayed
from a game won district or a regional cup
in the report filed by detective Wade

the fellow known as Ben suddenly turned up
to tell a tale of both his parents dead
the local vet who gave him a job one more dupe

to that double murder the orphan said
happened near Detroit when he was just 13
later a high school dropout he had hit the road

this town of thirty-five hundred taken in
by that vagabond arrested Monday on a burglary charge
had given him a standing ovation

at the ceremony for scholarship awards
as a senior his own a full one from A & M
graduated but then in Bryan a suspected robber of barns

here the vet still recalls the day he came
a clean-looking kid in need of a break
did well on any & every exam

his B.S. in animal science nothing fake
but with thieving & his mother alive in Poplar Bluff
rued that farewell barbecue    their putting of faith

in any such tragic past    more than enough
to warm Hill Country hearts now hard & cool
to the thought of growing ever again so generous

they & their applauding hands now feeling the fool
as for dad he only drove here to buy a necktie
his reason maybe as much against the Golden Rule

as the Michigan homicides in that drifter's lie
yet a father's ruse would make the trip come true
in a boyhood mind far simpler to justify

the family vacation in '48 to nearby Lake Bu-
chanan can always outweigh in any balance
his visit-to-a-dry-goods-store subterfuge

the alibi of a seller of life insurance
would be    as he told his boss    here on business
a week spent with wife kids cousins uncles & aunts

sleeping in a camper he'd bought for so much less
than he said it was worth though vented wrong
for any air to reach to that sweated thin mattress

on those sultry nights so hot so endlessly long
the hours an eternity awaiting signs of morning light
even dared to brave mosquitoes outside & watch for dawn

with every real or imagined sound or shadowy sight
beyond the yellow glow cast by that driftwood fire
drawing nearer to its needless heat in wondrous fright

preferred such fear to that closer safer trailer
later dad's scheme to load it with Christmas toys
hauled & peddled them house to house in a *Radio Flyer*

while he sold town to town his terms & twenty-pays
hitting the telephone operators & department stores
mother ever to remind him how only his boys

sold enough with innocent faces at neighbors' doors
to let him break even & empty that camper in time to move
to Altus where it disappeared though never from shores

have come to for this Vanishing Texas Cruise
forty years later a return trip to this river where
in its man-made lake the same sunken trees still seem to lose

another branch when limbs bob up as if for air
a rising to float at the rippled surface
as thoughts of a father & aunt both gone forever

ease up here in their boat to cast for crappie or bass
to set or check their trotlines by the lantern's light
as fluttering wings ping the Coleman's sooted glass

dying to enter its flame-filled bag still burning bright
on Rosalyn who suffered so many years before her end
fishing with Guy from Alaska to Amazon day or night

knew the deep seas from Azores to Thailand
wherever the Air Force stationed their handsome
son    dad testing irrigation canal or a farmer's tank

with his stinking balls of bait he would cook at home
caught nothing more exotic than gar or gasper-goo
lost minnows or worms to a mess of throwaway bream

hooked mostly mud or channelcats yellow or blue
but patient with pole & equally with rod & reel
while making his calls let wind carry a rubber balloon

out to the middle of that city lake these scenes reveal
here where Fall Creek has emptied for half-a-million years
in just one their count has doubled hear the tour guide tell

steaming by cliffs with claret cup cactus & prickly pear
on this beautiful 75 degree February day
the sky above the Colorado sunny & clear

on its 600 mile journey to Matagorda Bay
in the deepest spot he says the lake is 45 feet the river 12 to 15
this boat drafts 2 & a half comes equipped with a galley

Captain Al hopes he & Mike can spot a few of the 17
to 35 American eagles but fears the fishing fest
with its outboard motors may frighten them off    If golden

they're immature if black with white heads
full grown    They differ in their flat-winged
flight from the v-shaped wobble of buzzards build their nests

right on the ground & leave when these show up for eatin' rodents
& fish    Never kill no cattle though ranchers shoot the Bald
Confuse it with the Golden    Them there's double-crested cormorants

astompin' their feet & aflappin' their wings    On your left's
          Seldom Falls
one a their favorite haunts    The cedar here about's so thick
chokes out ranch grass    Resists any fire    Liveoak roots go tall

as the tree itself    Reach to the river down limestone strips
That great blue heron's astandin' in driftwood beer cans & trash
& that there's ball moss    It won't kill the tree    Lives on air like
          orchids

Up ahead before we turn around at Deer Creek we'll be apass-
in' Buzzard's Roost    yet dock without spotting wingspans 6 to 7 feet
drive back by outcrops of green glauconite & on to Burnet's

namesake where Elisa ran her four- & eight-hundred meters
at the gun sprinting for the tape    Burnet it was fired the very
          first shot
to free the whole South American continent    on her final
          kick beat

the field    won two medals even with shin splints    he
          forever boxed
in as when on her birthday May 20 underneath the
          brightest of stars
signed the Treaty of Velasco spared Santa Anna with all the
          others set

116

on stringing him up    after Miranda betrayed the
        revolution    Bolívar's
that is    David G. struck by pulmonary consumption &
        crossed the Sabine
in search of health    lived ten years with Comanches restored
        his vigor

avoiding ardent spirits subsisting on hunted game
said racing their favorite amusement their democracy
most perfect on earth little harmony in their deliberations

yet the vices of civilized life engrafted all too readily
who rescued that president-elect from a premature grave
later to preside over the first court session till the machinery

flat played out    his eldest lost in Civil War    poor &
        desolate yet saved
those horsemen's sounds for heavens plants & man:
*Muur paam-pee phee paa-ve Taa-ve*

*ha-nebe sau-nipp so-co-vete ta-bane tucan*
a "species" cut off who took him in they to "melt away
an untimely vernal snow inscrutable in their origin"

fluent in Spanish "unique in habits wild & uncultivated
but in no wise deficient in intellectual endowments"
"encroached" on at last by a "disastrous" race
        "*unsocial & depraved*"

both those & these proved gracious hosts    the difference
more in their guests    the one a wobbly errant bird
the other by generosity of spirit soared to eminence

as for dad if deceptive still he kept his word

## Bryan

this dead downtown recalls it all
farmers in Oshkosh-by-Gosh bib overalls
spitting on corners from plugs or dips
just yesterday sitting their green John Deeres
product of a blacksmith's shop in Grand Detour
with self-scouring disks as shiny & free of week-
day dirt as their half sun-reddened brows
all decked out for the ritual Saturday trip
to shop & see    swap talk of weather & crops
their fenced wagons parked at the local gin
their wire walls with bits of cotton clinging
as their bonneted wives waddle out & in
of the stores now rent for little when
the malls have closed so many doors
the Queen & Prince & Palace theatres
a royal history inherited by Chicano & Black
Woolworth's with nothing for five or ten
smelling of popcorn oil & Asian plastics

# Beaumont

## Goose Hunting

in whatever town have ended up
dreaming on cities free from fumes
of emissions from faulty systems
on every morning evening & afternoon
there's been a corner filling station
ready to assure would make it there

in Beaumont at Florida St. & Highland Dr.
the brick building built in nineteen-five
still housed in front the Brothers' Gulf
behind it the home where the one was living
when his oldest daughter took her holy vows
after the tennis star who had never failed

to rattle on for an hour of nothing new
the telephone switched from ear to ear
of her teenage smell married someone else
for lunch the other brother would walk a block
his wife preparing pasta with sweet fennel
or the goose with her son had legally shot

so high only their faint honking would signal
their Vs were over town & heading to feed
on rice the harvest combines had left behind
eating them would drop the pellets in plates
the wild taste cooked out by a family recipe
mother never learned & would as soon forget

had ever furnished it with such ingredients
would have legislators outlaw every gun
though each sneaks up upon himself   muddy
from keeping low   from crawling on elbows

until the flock was spread out thick & noisy
was close enough to stand & shoot    bloody

from the limit bagged    held by long warm necks
returned with spirits heavy as those sticky birds
yet knew without a share in the kill would miss
the meals    his mother in baggy hose    his father's
prayers    all three bowing & crossing themselves
could be she really did love Jesus just as well

*Class Reunion*

1

in a year marked by mountains &
mole hills    a waking each morning
to the real but postcard spectacle

of Popocatepetl    to the petty bribe
& a lawful yet unending heart-
rending romantic-socialist Mexican strike

sit down unready though desperate to write
of the Triangle City where two decades back
as a senior at South Park High

graduation came as a relief    a cocky farewell
like all the rest    though the last attended
other degrees taken    received by mail

though never achievement    its celebration
any feeling    any sense of completion
lost in the onward rush for spotting

some UFO of the soul later identified with
the poetic line & what María now calls
a Texas this memory has turned to myth

yet returning after twenty short years
may this private reunion remark how friends
have helped unknowingly shape an imaged ascent

may move them more than inscriptions they read
in the trophy case or that sad yearbook section
where few if any were chosen likely to succeed

2

a diabetic of the type
whose house & pockets
bulged with candy & cake

which he always shared
as he did of himself
but especially with those

new to the school which
made of strangers objects
for lunchroom ridicule

a kid with a stammer
one as shy as a girl
another too skinny for sports

all taken under G.A.'s wing
to feel at home
each other known

because of the boy
whose initials remained
as much a mystery

as his insulin need
a needle each day
of his oversweet life

too saccharine
for taste
or belief

3

good with cars
better with a beaker
best with words

in every case
wired or rigged
from Chemistry lab

where an evacuation after
his stink bomb fog
kept classes outside

for a heavenly hour
to Orchestra where he'd paper
his oboe or sax    for the

tuning of "boards"
served as his reeds    he as lead alto
to Speech where he'd read

in *U.S. News & World Report*
then change the facts or make up quotes
for a debate on the parity paid

so farmers didn't need to plant
at the contest eating an apple
biting down just as his opponent

went for a point    his serious side
ungraded though surviving
backfire laughter win or loss

4

too talented to give a hot damn
it all came
too easy to care

the beauty queens who called
or hung about as the tennis king
reigned on clay or asphalt court

the nonchalance of his passing shot
or at marching practice on the field
where he hurled his horn in the air

could play it better crumpled up
than those with dentless trumpets
giving it all they had

dressed like the rebel James Dean
with his ducktail & pants pulled low
cigarettes hidden from parents

a meek mother worshipped the earth
where he stepped danced outdid the rest
then gave it all up

took a refinery job like his dad's
the same father whose effusive love
shamed him in front of his friends

married a nobody plain & poor
rented a house happy as hell two blocks
from the home his genius had mocked

lefthanded yet rarely wrong    the trig &
calculus solutions coming out neat
proportioned as if from key-punch machines

though always touched by his Italian blood
a sensuous shape to the *a*s & *b*s
a pregnancy    a plump ripeness seemed

to grow on the page    in math
every problem taking on latinate life
his olive skin & glossy black brows

masking a mind mechanical as
DaVinci's    hiding perhaps a secret
as intriguing as his Mona Lisa's

yet the lines from his pencil or pen
never allowed nor given free rein
to roam beyond the algebra forms

& instead of drawing a dove in flight
drew a bead with his .410 gauge
followed red drops on leaves & grass

to a meadowlark dead in his bright-
yellow breast    though what was taken was
with grace withdrawn    ever so gently

even the feathers he felled appearing
to find pleasure    comfort in    the firm-
tender touch of his artist's pinpoint stroke

6

on tattered wallpaper hung photos of his father
riding in rodeos pictured atop his champion mount
holding up a blue ribbon in one hand a *Pabst*

in the other    sitting tall in the saddle    erect
& trim    a far cry from the broken paunchy little man
hanging about the matchbox house

with a hernia his hat on in pee-stained pants
cursing his dancer son for some effeminate fool
watched re-runs    Rockettes kicking in crotch-shot

rhythms    no son of mine muttered as he stared to where
the glazed bull horns stretched above their *Zenith* set
the choreographer-to-be eyeing the girls in gaudy drill

on downtown streets pausing before showcase windows
left untrimmed    bare models with contorted limbs
his own in imitation till he'd cackle aloud    pirouette a-

way    clipping out scenes from women's magazines
adding a caption to an ad of two facing kids
the unlikely boy releasing lines to an innocent mate

"I'll rip those pink panties to a shredded fringe
round your *Buster Brown* orthopedic saddle oxfords"
a humor horrifying his mother home from the beauty parlor

later to make his name in lights in old New York
touring with the Nikolai troupe to Italy & France
his mannikin body ridden    a bronc of modern dance

7

the class composer
his "Triple Double-Cross"
a one-man show

author of plot & script
producer director conductor
creator of sets & songs    copier of parts

a pure-blood Swede    an only son
born in New Gulf's Sulphur Camp
where his piano lessons began

his father walking in marshy land
looking out for nests of sky-blue eggs
checking the pipes carried in them

that hot yellow water    that devilish
mineral as if in veins    music the same
something worth selling body & soul

for hearing the chord
the overtone series could even reach
to a melody a harmony like Helen of Troy

ready to pay the price though fully aware
it might not work out as that musical he made
his three-act high school play

where the Broadway Shrew is tamed & won
following a trinity of double-crosses
willing still to score the piece at any cost

8

perennial winner as Miss Personality Plus
her limbs & features falling short of feminine
tall & big-boned was leader arbiter Christian

always called on to sing or pray
ever elected the president of society or club
her name synonymous with school spirit & love

though when it came to getting a date
for the Halloween dance hayride or game
her friends were faced with an impossible task

the boys they found willing were never her size
could only come up as far as her chin
in morals not even so high

surprising to all she eschewed a degree
thanked Daughters of Foreign & Revolutionary Wars
but could not accept their scholarship checks

took what her trio of girlfriends had sung
"A Sentimental Journey"    this as airlines stewardess
fulfilling a Methodist sense of service & fellowship

while the trio remarried & majored in Psych
she flew off to Atlanta Chicago New York
bending to businessmen with stiff drink & a smile

spending her layovers in every big city
rooming with Sappho's jet-age descendants
never once to shed a Mary Magdalene tear

9

in Salem she might have spent time in the stocks
been branded X-rated or charred at the stake
while in Beaumont was more than anything ignored

with her unshaven legs spread like a man's
sawing out-of-tune as last violin
though first in soccer beat hell out of all

with petticoats hiked    her muscled calves flexed
she outscored & kicked every male in the shins
bowling the Van Winkles over for a go-ahead goal

though her voice hardly lifted so any could hear
never absent    never late    faithful to the end
even at the prom her rose corsage failed to wither

as the unknown escort decked in a traditional tux
waltzed her about the ballroom in that low-cut gown
her longish hair by *Toni* or some spray-set brew

yet no medieval change rushed over her then
no frog leaped into being a center-fold bunny
no duckling molted into a kitten for *Gent*

only in puritan hearts of those who stared
struck by the lightning of their hidden regrets
shamed scarlet by thoughts had lodged & fed

stood judged of a hunting ugly as any
McCarthy managed on the star-chamber floor
sentenced to burn forever for having hoped her a

10

his voice pitched better for taffies & bees
always more at home hatching with hens
than in locker rooms coarse with jock itch & joshing

marched in his Greenie uniform like Oliver Hardy
his head thrown back    shoulders swung just so
a comic match in oversized shoes & bleached cross-straps

earned his way as head cashier at the Pyramid theatre
a drive-in rose before demolition from a marsh of mosquitoes
sold in boxes the black coiled repellent smoked & glowed

an incense for teenage neckers fogging their windows
while he preferred chatting & phone calls till closing
bachelor squaw in his glassed-in booth his cement tepee

would go out only with groups of girls for cherry cokes
chummy more with his mother & the one true church
than any of his own age    his own or the opposite sex

practiced his clarinet religiously for the solo contest
preparing himself to direct one day the public bands
to receive each September new family members

kids nurtured by a spinster who hears confessions
dreams    disappointments    hatreds    crushes
sharing with them anything but a pallet or bed

on weekends driving 200 miles home to attend a service
to his mother's hip    to help her down steps    the trips
retold hours on end    how she nearly talked his ears off

11

at the speech tournament in New Orleans
on finding they'd gone for drinks to Pat O'Brien's
had taken in jazz & the girlie shows

then sprayed his hotel bed with *Burma Shave*
he offered up for the earth's poor sinners
one of his special patented prayers

& as he clasped his manicured fingers
pursing his lips in supplication
he heard a laughing off of under-aged asses

slender & tall with a pure complexion
of peaches & cream    his long auburn hair
curled in a cowlick by a last florid twist

in girls' rooms his comb ever craved by mirrors
by bobbie-soxers swooned for the saintly crooner
his benedictions driving lipstick to muss his picture

in the business world a cinch for getting ahead
an administrator or top official    in job interviews
with former classmates to chuckle up a sleeve

all the right equipment    looks brains ethics
an orphan son who proved their trust
his adoptive parents just proud as punch

though never forgiven by the giggly bunch
married nightwatchmen or used car lots
his angel face still pillowed where husbands

12

their white frame house freshly bordered in black
the shingled roof of a purplish-greenish cast
glittering at rare angles from sun's rise or set

the dark stale sofa sighing odors from out of the past
so discouraging to those had come to pick her up
who after one date would never come back

her sixty-fivish father a survivor his wife as well
two taciturn strangers she met at those garden meals
kept them at a safe distance by her highest of grades

wore even then in a year of hot blinding pink
her charcoal skirts with white starched collars
then a touch of make-up showed up of a sudden

lent to cheeks a bloom late as their second child
in blouses still buttoned up to ruffles at her neck
her dove-soft breasts fluttering fuller at every breath

in easy subjects her concentration beginning to wane
as her moon-faced looks wakened the nodding rooms
her voice going softer as her marks were starting to fall

& though her name still made each honor roll
the knifed toilet walls knew her initials too
her salutatory address penned anxious for a ring

the promised phone call   answered   then the glitter gone
her college career eclipsed by an infant's cries
taken in to echo colorless in that reticent home

13

Saturdays she rushed from popcorn to imitation pearls
making change at registers in the downtown variety store
later ran off not customers but a lovesick boy

she the middle daughter of a Lutheran minister
played organ at church     first violin in orchestra
planned to continue her studies but in some other place

& as she told him who waited at evening worship
stood about till her breaks at the 5 & 10
she was just wanting to have a little fun

popcorn first     only later a diamond
sat parked in his car at the parsonage curb
or kissed him fully on her front porch swing

hanging close in his arms at their senior prom
her faint perfume pressing him even harder
with visions of her soul virgin forever

never her match at the same seventeen
his mind set on romance     hardly on sex
more on how he could wed her training

how Luther's hymns must purify limbs
a father's sermons sanctify the lowest of thoughts
had missed the moral of her simple calling

gave him the register run-around bag-to-string routine
no knots nor honey in June   knew soon enough it would be
a conservatory in Kansas   her ministry of music

14

was meant for the Navy
any branch or field
where factoring's out

though capable of math & in fact
he could worry any problem
half to death     though never quite

for nothing with him was ever finished
the elementary mattering far more
than any solution could make the grade

while others found the product
hardly worth the effort
he would fail to give it up     ever

insisted on knowing the reason
when who could care less
since the invention

installed in every home
served the purpose     worked
was explained in any text

a dunce only in the way
his face drew a blank
his feet came flat

though none of this to keep him
out of the service     yet just in case
stationed nowhere real strategic

15

his father's pirogue he riveted after his work
that metal job they tipped over to fall in together
swamping it to save a dog could swim

phoned him at home to say it was tangled up
in trotlines & lilies    never quite able
to go it alone    another simple lesson

like where without them would this poetry be
or missing the rest    those never known
or not nearly so well    but fell in with

struggling together in the current rage
flailing about    drag racing    sneaking a fag
caught on hooks set for others    chicken livers

or fell for flowers    those closed to as if by night
though later they too would think it over
finding love    here at high tide    gone at low

not that any would make it better or change his ways
why even bother them back    how ever measure
the lives meant little or far too much

to learn how promise & expectation could go astray
how in dropping bones had grabbed for less
how back then nothing could prove great enough

yet so certain would take the biggest dare
in the end afraid to brave a friend's own face
go down together against that hooded cross-town rival

16

This Is Your Life     a poetry show
brought to you by Paradox & Chance
emceed by Terza     the Star of Stanzas

transportation provided by Image Airways
accommodations arranged by Diction & Rhyme
wardrobe courtesy of Symbol Incorporated

all these lives were produced & directed
by those who furnished their form & spirit
by teachers whose classes opened & filled

still indebted to those who made it happen
equally to those who made it impossible
forced a reconsideration     to renewal of faith

still deeply grateful to each scribbled wall
to bannered steps     lockers bent & pictured
English & typing tests every lab & practice-hall

but most of all owe a special thanks
to those who appeared to bring it back
the screams & tears when the curtain parted

& could see at last the Lives Have Led
heard again the storied days they generously gave
hearts have touched one's into feeling

to this & more bid fond farewell
till same teenage hour same graduation
wishing the years to come will enrich as these

*Jazz God & Freshman English*

Harold T. Meehan:

from that day you entered the band hall
looking for a 3rd-chair for replacing Wayne
still sitting at the time eleventh in line
this hearing ever since hasn't been the same

prayed for real that every better player
would turn down that lowest of parts
in practices held before or after classes
for the one big blast each spring & fall

not counting the autumn Friday nights
for football sock hops on lips so shot
from marching & blowing half-time shows
till at last you arrived at the awaited name

o perfect you never were
far from it the way you'd breathe
after a soccer game of fifty minutes
from being winded by the fags you'd puff

or once on leaving your jumbled home
quietly without a word the record going
you on the couch passed out from mixing
vodka with the bebop licks of Dizzy & Bird

when the couples wanted the band should do
current hits like Elvis' *Hound Dog*
you'd give them *Stars Fell on Alabama*
& plenty of whispered go-to-hells

after rehearsing dull trios of Irons & Sousa
you offered the miracle of Beethoven's First
the puzzling wartime Fifth of Shostakovich
even *Lust for Life* with Quinn & Douglas

that film seen with string & stageband teacher
the night you drove over to a student's home
imagine a grown man inviting a sophomore
a pimply-faced player was seated last chair

being lowered together down creaking mines
to tulip rows sprouted from oil paint tubes
squeezed by some guy unknown before
some Vincent Van Gogh sliced off his ear

then classics through the bore of a Bach 7C
as lips touched to life a metal mouthpiece
a Martin horn unlocked by your magic key
that opened up a world of unending sound

o invitation to more than music or movie
from sunflowers ragged on canvas stalks
but a mirror's thickness to poetry's others
hang heavy forever in Blake's eight lines

his words would release to dreams of love
to the writing & revising deep in the nights
for appearance in magazines so unheard of
closed down as would be South Park High

& the grade
o yes had almost forgotten
the course went for
no credit

Rev. Elwood J. Birkelbach:

no recliner no rocker
could hold you still
your back forever a pain
your brain as restless

as when it worked into a Sunday sermon
Goethe's transcendental image of God
sleeping in the earth & stones until
dreaming in flowers He awakes in man

your second floor study so dark & heavy
with the books & books on the inscrutable Will
Brother Lawrence's letters Luther's Reformation
Aquinas & Wesley & the mental health guides

climbed your stairs as if to Mount Sinai
up Kierkegaard's mountains in Moriah
in your pulpit appeared a burning bush
sweating & swaying & reddening with

the remembered weight of your steamy nights
on South Sea isles    your tours in World War Two
as chaplain to troops there after the Jap
your German-Texan ears made captive

by the tale of a tribe transposed itself
from Brazil or Venezuela
retaining in miniature
that nation's shape

as it landed in the blue Pacific
made safe from those alien spears
finding peace through telepathy    you never
always & ever shifting in comfortless armchairs

in the end seeking relief in an insurance firm
from a body & mind
too huge for a church
shrunk by the tithes that bind

Professor Francis E. Abernethy:

propped on a classroom desk
the lace workboots never quite going with
your youthful face nor the old man's tie
with your talk of Sputnik & a Cellini brag

nothing in your office
ever quite matching
a Beowulf drawing beside
rattlesnakes curled in glass

Mickey Spillane in one breath
Jonathan Swift in the next
then off on field trips spelunking
or taping folk tunes from sixteen-three

ballads surviving
from Shakespeare's day
in sleepy towns like Kountze Sour Lake or
Buna

no Mahon nor native pecan
yet a Texan from the Piney Woods
& so would set you down
here as if in gumbo earth

that you give again
of caves that throng
with serpents & song
stalagmites that turn into satellites

as your heroes old & new
come & go
in cow-caked Justin kangaroos
quoting Benvenuto

*A Little Something For William Whipple*

1

back & forth on the criss-crossing walks
building to brick building of then Lamar Tech
changing of classes in a blinding white light
no St. Paul just a coastal sun in summer
or choking from the smog & fumes drifted in
from adjacent refinery or the sulphur pits
sat reading beneath those stunted loblolly
unreached to rooftops of gravel & tar
all a veritable Garden
at the very least a Texas Eden

where library assignments you made
even now with a Ph.D.
still wouldn't pass such tests
climb to heights your search required
newspapers from Boston in '73
an obscure note on Poe in French
couldn't find them to save one's soul
boiling then in your scholarly hell
shoulder to the research stone
only to have it roll back down

when in from humid heat to freeze between
the refrigerated stacks & colder stares
from a lady librarian at the reference desk
trying again & again to discover at last
the why of Doctor Johnson's long fear of death
while a yellow fog engulfed the campus    filled
the halls    was Heavenly
& just to breathe the novels
you taught in a huff
worth finishing with a stigma C

2

to your office as to an altar would come
offering the lines like a newborn lamb
words as thick with symbols as wool on a winter ram
till you sheared the fluff   whole stanzas   even the one
had arrived so wondrously alive   miraculously
mysterious as any ewe seen dropping her young
from a study of sonnets had made an innocent song
only to have you leave it standing unsteady ugly

then found it to be the fittingest gift
when you deigned to slit the bleating verbose
penciling a loved metaphor & saying flatly it go
even thanked lucky stars whenever you missed
deep midnight thoughts had saved from despair   grateful for
wrenching of tender phrases any daring page's crumpled horn


3

& so will the debt endure forever
why is it your image of that mantelpiece
means more than have managed in all these years
were the glass figurines ocelots or leopards
they remained a menagerie of burnished words

though reading that poem after marriage & degrees
would fail to find any sleekness there
feared admit it had been a mere period piece
its diction had seemed so modern in tone
just imitative & yet had driven on

& still the flame & mirror of its memory
shine finer than any have cast
or that simple but subtle living room scene
though perhaps no setting you even composed
is yet the sum have deeply owed

with dreams of giving an aura only
half the glow that printed fireplace gave
would return as reflection has for all these years
on critics you quoted on your encouraging curse
some ember of that matchless verse

*Hustling Shuffleboard With Hearts-&-Flowers Harold*


Beeson
better known as the
Beast

from his acned face
& physique
like a bouncer's from across

Beaumont's railroad tracks
at the College St. Flamingo Club
made all the county beer joints

just after classes
on Hemingway & Faulkner
ordering only *Jax*

that New Orleans
Cajun brew
sprinklng a sandy stuff

on varnished boards
caressing long piano player's
fingers round a metal puck

sliding it along the flesh-colored
wood    back & forth a bit
getting the feel & angle

to hang it off the edge
or give the sucker's a
click would send it

sailing for the gutter
& take him for a 5 or 10
high-tailing it out of there

if & when the guy wised up
& decided all of sudden
to go for a gun

or like the night
a dozen rough-necks
off the tower shift

went for him in sawdust
after he'd crunched a cheater's ribs
up against a washbowl

on the humid wall
of that house converted
to a cockroach bar

or shot through the underarm
running from a sheriff's raid
out the backdoor to

sweetgum & pine
what little he made
going for booze

& poetry books
elected J.P. in
of all places

Rose City Texas

*Carroll Black: Author of* Stephen Hero

who came to Lamar Tech from Orange
a city just inside the Texas line
that invisible border through bayous
stretching beyond into Cajun wilds

his hometown reached by a highway
lifted up & over the Neches River
tankers below heading out for the Gulf
or inland to port as they floated beneath

that "rainbow" bridge with its black gold view
to scummy reeds    at night the soaring flames
burning off gas    nothing close to his prose
his retouched portraits of Dedalus or Bloom

for even as a freshman his one ambition
to write another *Ulysses*
how he'd found the classics    reared in swamps
the biggest mystery of that mystical year

mother swore his underwear were trimmed with lace
the Ds he made in German bothered much more
couldn't equate his Buck Mulligan manner with
the grades he pulled    on clarinet seated last chair

but from here he comes in clear    waiting for class
leaning in the hall    in that same black rayon suit
silk white shirt    re-reading *Dubliners* or *Leaves of Grass*
the nearest thing to Joyce's hero Lamar Tech knew

introduced Faulkner & the latest MJQ
loaned the *Fontessa* album said Listen to
their Harlequin piece It's the greatest hit
The Commedia dell' Arte through a jazz quartet!

Those four Blacks in tails with their delicate touch
are reviving the Italian Renaissance in bluesy tones
heard it echoed off walls of neighboring homes
where crews half-slept till the graveyard shift

spinning the record past two a.m.
repeating how dull those schoolmates were
applying to each all that author had meant
so certain had awakened at Finnegan's words

to a tower overlooked the pains of love
a jetty built by the winds of wits
books piled for the crossing to Paris
exile    definition    refinement    horse piss!

since then have been    not there    but abroad
& it just ain't so    homesick    confused
tortured by doubt    the natives intimidating
their chants of hands-off politics

no sensitive lines came easy or tough
just a picture of that Liberal Arts hall
superimposed while riding crushed in a bus
straining to catch at the quick foreign phrase

wondering where he was    how the novel progressed
thought of Pierre Menard rewriting Cervantes
curious if Carroll had done it to "The Dead"
was still continuing then to imitate Yeats

haunted still by his talk of the Irish greats
still warmed by memories of a *Portrait's* first page
till remembrance went cold as baby tuckoo's bed sheet
hopeless as that blind block of North Richmond Street

yet revisited & believed in those Beaumont scenes
of him lounging in the hall with its lighting dim
off discolored walls & unbuffed floors
the books in his hands held mostly for looks

though still letting in as if through a door
to the wonder of this    a place to fit
a form to fill    boiling of crude down to a fuel
the cleansing ethyl for an art to steer

gaining for one raised on bayou or marsh
faith in the refinery as an image can mean
though what he opened stayed closed to him
with his dreams of novels unsoiled by the near

now feeling it deeper than ever    the failure
of this poem he deserves in return
hope at least for a fellow who led the way
the cliché may follow    'tis better to give than etcetera

# Austin

*Proem*

at the center    at the heart
of how & why have been & are
garden of wrongs must still recall

the seat of law & a greed feeds on
site come true from his "academy scheme"
Estevan's dream in '33

of a campus    of a where to sit & listen
at the feet of a Boatright Dobie or Webb
professors of a faith in that frontier way

vouched from a time of toughing it out
have longed somehow to touch
without a loss of here & now

their talk of cutting-horse lariat & brand
sixshooter axe & bowie-knife blade
windmill "bull wheel" cable or bit

simple tools proved so titan in hands
of men & women grown heroic-wise
in a prose of writers but rarely known

sensing none alone if not all together
might reach so deep to a meaning sought
no wildcatter logging the signs so well

could read the core & tell for certain
had come at last to salt or sand
awaiting still the drill could strike

right for singing in stratum or source
would never so soon run dry
a lease longer than for cattle or crude

would return Estevan's lay of the land
when he mapped its channels & bays
nearer his call for courses to take

in English Spanish & French
his belief in a credit line based
on what each man has said he'll do

at the very least to avow the debts
to summon up & render accounts
name teachers & mates

the dividends from a rented room
a class attended
memorial halls

memoried haunts
wins & losses
at stadium or court

the leaf- & creek-veined hills
of pecan cedar & oak
have soaked like rain

have burned like sun
remembered rays now magnified
held to the page to blaze for him

who started upon the straight & error
paved the way for bones & blood
laying the slab & cornerstone

for every feeling & thought
for 300 yearly shining days
paying the toll & utility bill

in his dank Inquisition cell
defrayed with the coin
of a gnawing doubt

with visions sired
these daily scenes
east & west on 11th Street

of blacks still down & out
of hooker bars & liquor stores
at a mere two blocks' remove

from the final resting place
from his Peach Point grave
the remains uprooted

interred in this the State maintains
his statue in bronze by Coppini
his right & dark-green outstretched hand

extended yet toward all he hoped
would be achieved
to the ills he'd not conceived

in his left a scroll unrolled
for all to read
epic of an entrepreneur

while at his back
the cape in folds
drapes to his founding feet

as he stares away
to the bier in white
the barred encased & sculpted corse

of Albert Sidney Johnston
commander fell at Shiloh
directing his Rebel troops

whose ears
were it not
for that stronger stop

than the glass's pane
than the ironwork grate
would yet take in

the humble hymns
from the Shiloh Baptist choir
rise nearby & never falter

while Estevan stares to where
his indecision led
to racial slurs & bloodied fields

to where his insight failed
to where if now he looked behind
with eyes at the back of his head

could spy across in littered yards
his slavery's kids ride metal scraps
roll tires or toss their airless balls

yelling jive in a grammar broken
as half their project homes
where just next door

his Mexican heirs
will ever insist
he stole it all

down their beers to polkas
*corridos* blasted out
on stereo tapes in lowered cars

in blouses loud
with red & pink
in frayed workshirts hung out to dry

from a dead mesquite (or so it seems)
a chinaberry with its inedible fruit
their wet weight swinging on plastic lines

has sagged them down
lives of those
must still bear up

strive at greening deep within
with a sap will flesh
the yellow seed

these sagging stanzas from seeing him
dragged in dirt
though each has need

of knowing earth
the bitter taste
of where it is he's

gotten off
deserves no greater blame
no stain for what was tried

tarnish *sí* on his "violet crown"
O'Henry's phrase
for this city's sunset sky

LBJ on touring 6th
had seen them there
in '38 in full view then

of the legislative lawns
40 families to a single lot
watched them as from a single faucet

each carted water a hundred yards
one leaky tub to wash them all
an eyesore in Lyndon's House report

a crying shame so near he said
to this tallest capitol dome
its very edifice set

on a chalk named after & for
Estevan's patient steady ways
no shale that swells when wet

shrinks when dry
& by geologist Flawn's account
the cause of most

foundation cracks
while this holds firm
won't shift about

& warp the floors     those at 24th
sloped where Stine Rudin & Reck
ate what Don the trumpeter fixed

pasta on the old "Detroit Jewel"
his test for when
the spaghetti cooked

slinging a gob
against the wall
to see it stick

didn't on that moral
racial stand
waffled about unlike his stone

sold that laboring race
the real for higher stakes
though a rub can yet return

the magic gleam of all he gave
his trip to Vera Cruz
from Matamoros took the cruise

at his own unreckoned cost
his wardrobe prairie bare
worn out long for those

stayed safe at home
yet swore he'd kept
prime acres for his own

no house no wife
uncaressed by an Elisabet Ney
who washed him Ivory white

chiseled him out
in his modest suit
her favorite horse

its hide converted to
a mattress stuffed
with duckling down

molded from
her Artie's face
a mask before

she burned
to ash
his tender form

was not to meet this man she made
his hands warm or cold never to know
her black inviting shag of hair

in death his gaze still fixed upon
Johnston here below
the sleeping soldier

his wounded frame
turned by Elisabet's hammered touch
to a picture of painless rest

while only through Coppini eyes
the look her rival lent to him
can Estevan view her masterpiece

his glance as far from her own art
as his frail figure from
her Bismarck's vigorous bust

her first big break as sculptress
Estevan only coming after
her long line of Europe's minds

a grudging Schopenhauer
agreed to a sitting even as
Garibaldi Wagner & Grimm

then made her way
through a secret wedding on Madeira Isle
to the climate of a Georgia farm she hoped would cure

her consumptive husband-lover
then on here with him
to Six Shooter the junction where

diphtheria carried off her little son
later to her medieval castle
her Hyde Park miniature

where Estevan came to her fingers' feel
though in his dreams she'd not appear
never to lie with him in cell 15

as cold there as Johnston in repose
o what a comfort she could have been
to one ensnared by deadly men

came instead
to dress him in
a buckskin coat

its sleeves with a fashionable fringe
leaned at his side
a flintlock so admired

by crowds vacation here
stepping easily from seal to seal
of Alamo Goliad & San Jacinto

commemorated all in gold
"the large hearts of heroes"
forced marches & firing squads

on the rotunda's marble floors
walk at ease from past to present
gaze upon each polished plate

each governor's date
from daguerreotype to kodacolor
though hardly suspect

this is the man
the one with the effeminate face
so short & thin

shouldered the load
of a warring quill
after vetoing arms year after year

wrote to Mary of the carnage
of thousands slaughtered
another Iliad in every age

of the applause for military braid
while the bloodless pioneer
with his cause of cotton & corn

reaped no parades nor holidays
though here & there a woman's won
Albert Sidney's wife who sketched

a picket fence
centered upon the page
on paper still unfallen

the legislature as it was in '52
with a horse-drawn carriage in front
a dog behind with his tail still up

off to the right a cabin of logs
on it flying yet a one-star flag
this city before that Civil War

when before her haughty husband's fall
Custer's wife sat down to write
of streets with armed & roaming youths

duels & feuds & rage
her words outlasting
bullets bombs & agent orange

such women might have saved it from
such foolish ways
María too    then & now

& which of these framed here
elected to a term or two
in sessions long or short

has added even
one iota to
the law he lived

the vote his prison vision cast
for love & trust
for a fertile thought

would bring the harvest in
one these circular walls
can even now retain

echoing with youthful sound
as the All-City Orchestra performs
a music Mary & Estevan should've heard

did in their own prophetic ways
their lives in concert then
as now these brass & winds

percussion harp & strings
among them Darío's violin
playing for a delayed broadcast taping

Estevan put off & shut away
no camera nor sensitive mike
to catch him in that silent cell

these his measures nonetheless
the Handel composed as if for him
these his own uplifting strains

Humperdinck's his evening prayer
a pantomime of Gretel wherein
each student forms a leading part

directed by Estevan's pen-baton
guided by his steadying beat
through & to a final score    a bill run up

can never settle    parents & issue ever
owing for the privilege in tune or out
for auditions won by son or daughter

his answer to
all & more than here
any session has passed or ever will

than a single man can hope to leave
each generation the offspring of
his imprisonment & failing health

this tall rotunda ringing with
his notes & jottings there in jail
taken with a hidden stick of lead

thrummed his cell's aeolian bars
with now a harmony
still reaching here

up & up tier after tier
to where each governor's term
needs first & last to learn his letters

each & every one by heart
recite his thankless thirteen years
translating deeds to wilderness lands

his work with foreign words
the Spaniard's richest gift
a treasure yet distrusted

still suspected as a Catholic plot
thinking the worst at its open tones
funny trills of that neighbor's tongue

took from the first to be his own
spoke it to plead his Colony's case
that distant government's good

to see them settled
to have them thrive
traveling there to find

as if the victim of an enchantress' spell
his six-day trip upon the Gulf
transformed into a seasick month

in Jalapa his journey slowed again
where Perry the historian-dean accepted
another post when that union strike

ended a promising permanent position
had sold the furniture & appliances for
at prices so low María swore "you gave them all away"

then puzzled out which way to head
Albuquerque    anywhere she said but Texas
loathed yet knew the chances better

loaded the car    the kids unseen
from plants & cartons piled to the roof
crying not to leave their pet white pigeon

limped out through a monsoon rain
after a Pemex station the motor missing
with no protective overhang

water having dripped into the tank
in hysterics when Darío locked himself
wept inside through that restroom door

on to spend a restless night in Poza Rica
fearful attendants would break & steal
moving on next day to needless worry

hearing in each sound the engine fail
stranded in the big middle of nowhere
then made it to the Gulf's aromatic air

to the calming beach at Tampico
to a hostel by the laving waves
fried redfish & a good night's sleep

then back on the road to Matamoros
passing through customs & crossing over
drove to a motel would take no check

to sleep upright at a roadside park
to awake wornout & stiff    half starved
at dawn to slide the side door back

to find if the kids had ever slept
watched helplessly as her *Café de oro*
her four jars of instant coffee

rolled out & broke upon the ground
the glass & grains so quickly swept
by a puff of morning breeze

all those Mexican prospects
gone with the wind
a Bogart film in the Sierra Madre

those emptied bags of gold dust
blown & scattered mixed with sand
then arrived at last in the heat of August

o murderous month when tempers flare
after the long hours at office desks
to stall & steam in Mo-Pac traffic

home to stuffy air-conditioning
to plumbing in bathrooms
backing up

cooped up kids turned into imps
tormenting the one & only mother
of this their one & only life

lose the facts in dog-days heat
husband & wife
their fire put out

rekindle it here
at Barton Springs
their drive renew

by a dive into
the cool clarity of
this public pool

here too at Zilker Park
his legacy coming clear
in its cold solace from summer's hell

nerves soothed by wading in
as too the memory of that Mexican nightmare
recalls the one he knew

held up by the rebels' roadblock
by his passport a General
failed to endorse

as June to August had awaited too
those papers' "final stamp"
came at last by train to the Distrito Federal

to be met by the Sullivans & ride with them
up & over mountains to that Cholula home
by the pyramid plundered by Hernán Cortés

to the cobblestones of intimate streets
in the faculty's exclusive compound
Universidad de las Américas

an eden at the feet of snow-capped peaks
volcanic twins Popo & Ixtaccihuatl
Orizaba's outline in the distance dim

came to discover was seated atop
resentments ready to erupt
dropped in a lavabed of envy & spite

treated him as an animal
a criminal thrown
headlong in jail

had gone an agent
to petty sides
then & there that very thought

caught in the midst of teachers played
with a dictatorial president
at their losing political game

their flags flown from barricades
sign of a faculty had taken control
the administration driven to Puebla

though never for long
the last word ever the purse strings'
professors armed but with symboled armbands

with academic freedom's weak demands
with each campus brigade bearing the name
of some famed & martyred Marxist

instead of passing commands
from man to man
walkie-talkies

used binoculars to read
on a truck at the gate
its letters three-feet tall

"Open please, gas man"
fearful the students of engineering
might storm their chainlink fence

reliving the Revolution
in their khaki pants
he loyal

before & after
& had come to serve
to assure those ran the land

his colonists all
were only afraid
of Indian raids

missed their slaves
appealed not to be
under Coahuilan rule

& for fixing their eternal feuds
deciding their mean disputes
defending rightful claims

of some only bought to sell
received no other recompense
than a prisoner's peso a day

used to bribe the guard on duty
to bring him a copy
of Plato in French

said bread & water
taken with books
beat any monarch's regal meal

yet in confinement poisoned by
a diet missed    the one craved all his days
with dialogue there reduced

to his own
one-sided voice
with his cave

an allegory of
his own betrayed
imprisoned state

chained while those behind his back
worked their bag of shadowy tricks
fingers in the form of ferocious dogs

or rattlers poised to strike
to cast aspersions
false reports

bound there
to take as true
their insubstantial blame

deprived him of
the burning light
of a summer's day

fed his hungering mind
on every glimmering fear
though praising still

beyond the rest
those had caged him in
the Mexican

since Adam & Eve
as a work unmatched
of grand & noble design

a popular government liberal & free
a denial of all divinity
despotic greed

writes with passion
from his sunless cell
declares the unlettered nation

a retarded sad affair
in '32 had entered his plea
to free the press

against those argued it best to wait
till schooling of an ignorant mass
could ready it for the printed page

*esto seria lo mismo*
*que encerrar á uno*
*que tenia ojos debiles*

*en un cuarto enteram<sup>te</sup> obscuro*
*sin un solo rayo de luz*
*con el fin de prepararle*

*para aguantar la luz brillante del sol—*
*es decir debilitar la vista mas*
*bajo el pretesto de fortalizarla*

registering another month & day
recording in his dim-lit dungeon
an earthquake beyond the Richter

in his booklet overlooked
by friskers confiscated
his few effects

only a pencil to overcome
betrayal by those at home
happy to have him out of the way

those unwittingly sent to him
his violent visitation      his vision of
this city of learning & light

before its coming would feel himself
a crust of earth torn apart by pity
his own a nature too quick to serve

at the beck & call
of friend & foe
had pitched him out      had locked him up

in his darkness of night & day
a Russia under Peter the Great
its lone seaport at Archangel

iced over half the year      "a giant
closed up in a cave with only
a pinhole"      Estevan's one escape

his being borne on wings
of its skylight angle above
to soar through a five-hour reading space

to contemplate    then down again
to breathe his lonely landscape
its damp adobe    its walls smudged

with an earlier inmate's sole release
his serpent drawn entwining
a Genesis tree

its crude & smutted fruit
become an image of
all he feels he's yet produced

trapped for weeks
then let out unexpectedly
with a sentinel to guard

for an hour's walk
back to 1574
the same courtyard

saw performed
the Inquisition's auto-da-fé
its public burning & spectacle

where now but a single tree
flames upon his sudden sight
its bonfire of brilliant green

& near it still more dazzling
a fountain shoots its liquid sparks
blinding to one grown overlong

accustomed only to mud & dark
feasts now on the water's fronds
leaves flashing with reflected light

crystal limbs receive the day
then let it fly
as birds will enter & dart away

his mind lifting before
its pillar stands aglow
tall in the brightness

of its tumbling flow
a shining strength
could raise the barrenest state

nourish its roots
from head to foot
pour forth in every despair

regains his spirit
in the open air
a freshness fills his lungs

free at last from cell 15
then abruptly locked back in
returned to that serpent's den

where tremors rock his cot
the snake's head beginning to sway
the poisoned apples to bob

till he speaks aloud
to the venomous shades
to all his persecution's long aroused

What temptations can a place possess
Or is it false hope in where we go
Turns bitter the plants we long to bless?

Had it been I removed there only to know
The liveoak for its grotesque shape,
Its giant shadow 'gainst summer's Vulcanic blow—

Packed in no plans the pigmy-minded ape
Can ever plumb, lugged along no dreams a small-
Ness misapprehends, held no land to a promise never made—

Would I lie here now an Icarus in his fall,
Brought low by those have clipped these pinions
Were spread to fly them higher? O the ingrates all!

Have let dear Sister down. What sacrifice, what privation
To follow me, and now her trust has turned to grief.
And Mary Holley's plan to bring her son.

This too heaps coals upon my head. There's no relief
For me, nor was for her in all that heat. Her trip
To Brazoria when the towboat smoked, the cabin leaked,

Her vessel moving so slowly it seemed a spectre ship,
Her berth as much a coffin as here this cell.
I see her now the way I never shall, her slip

In the oppressive noonday sun fallen from a pale-
Ness only Horace knew, her stockings in breezeless air
Rolled from where . . . I have no right. That way lies hell.

But where else am I then? Is it not this lair
They've holed me in? Better had it been to live in sin
Than serve without a woman's love and hear them swear

That all I've done was meant for me, for Austin,
Who must be watched, suspected now of mil-
Lions hoarded, a fortune faraway in some Virgin-

Ia bank. Made in slag perhaps, had Papa stuck with lead. The wil-
Derness brought his end quicker than shot from any mine.
Returned from Bexar so fatigued, so weak and ill

That all the blood his doctor let was drawn in vain.
That journey did him in, and now my own has turned me in a
    single year
A misanthrope. Came to settle them all on the grant he gained,

Gone with not a thing to show, his indebtedness still uncleared,
Deserted by Kirkham coming back, the powder in his gun
Wet with rain, could kill no squirrel, no deer.

Living off acorns, berries, roots, Richmond
His slave exhausted the same as the horse and mule,
Abandoned him down the Sabine. Phillip the 2nd
   submitted his son

To death at the hands of the Inquisition. His religious zeal
Above and beyond paternal love. O slavery's the curse
Of curses! The robust tireless black, his story so unreal,

Too real to hear. And mine. My Colony's slave I am,
   chapter and verse.
And how could I say of the decrepit negro woman I own
She's not worth keeping, who's softened my clothes with harsh-

Est lye, her ladled recipes the sole feminine touch I've known.
Have followed his deathbed wish, never to let him down.
Am so by friends on either side. My love for the Mexican

Proof to the colonists I have sold them out,
My service to those taken here as treason, to these worse
Than murder. This government tires me now,

Have had more respect for it than it's yet deserved,
But now I'm done with that. You're too impa-
Tient, he said. You want to go too fast. How not prefer

Her round full face,
Soft as an autumn moon,
Her warmth and eastern grace,

To hear and see again and soon
Her light pink lips, her open mouth,
Her hands at the keyboard or about the guitar, embracing  the tune,

"Pensez a moi" . . .

& do
down every street
these thoughts of you
on walking Shoal or Waller Creek

nights relived on Hickey's screened-in porch
at 23rd & Rio Grande
a visit spent at 24th
among musician friends of Andy's

in every garage apartment lived
on Poplar over Bracker    at San Gabriel
back of Faulkner    on Sabine above Red River
with Rudin & King   house-shoed Raja Rao passed on Pearl

by the littered crumbling Wooten House
with its crape myrtles
overgrown    its azaleas the city's first set out
fluted stone columns with Ionic capitals

cut by an artisan-carver "incarcerated
for drunkenness"    on the doctor's word paroled
to work on his home where alkies now are recuperated
redeemed by walls & gardens DeLois restored

along the way to the best of dentists
Gerald Latimer up West 19th    changed to MLK
with the snipping of his thread in Memphis
by a sniper in this nation's pay

"The Plantation of Stafford just
above Bolivar was sold
to Mr. Neal of Natches—
including 20 negroes"

through it all to find in you
a hero for this or any time
then arrive a romantic wrecked anew
by head-ons in a realist mind

yields but a one-way turn
back to that solitary confinement cell
there at least have safely earned
a right to hear your Jacksonian tale

Even before I came, Britain Baily had settled there.
Some said he had come from Kentucky, though who
Could tell with Captain Brit, a character

If ever there was. The cholera in '32
Put to rest his dubious claims. But then not all.
He had his land, that Brazos plot, his own place where to

Breathe his last, whose walls
He'd squared and chinked, trued as best a forger could,
His wife beside him when he died. And this recalls

Not alone
What little there is to show—a bed
Shared with each year putting wed-

Lock off,
Another's sof-
Ter, fragrant arms,

Her comfort and her charms
Still withheld,
Postponed, delayed until

This thankless job,
This labor has robbed
Me long, is once and for all over and done—

But how she carried out his strange request. Declared he wouldn't
Stoop to any man, never had, was not about to in the grave.
Bid her have him buried upright, at the bottom put

Some whisky, his rifle in his grip, keep the coffin erect,  to face
It west, to the setting sun, the direction journeyed
All his days. And so she did, had the hole dug just the way

You would a well, and lowered him in feet first. Asserted,
Aside from having always stood, and the rights he swore a squat-
Ter holds to land he's come to know, title or no, a third

Claim, if further from the truth, yet closer to what
I have ever held, the view says credit must reside
Not in banks but men, not in property goods or chat-

Tel slaves, but what a man has said he'll do, his pride
In how it's done, the word he gives, the stand he takes,
Never in history's chances will choose up warring sides

And trap one in between. Am caught by hate
On either hand, disowned, mistrusted by the very crowd
Am in their service to represent. It breaks

A heart like his, or makes it find in fraud
A blessedness. When word first came how in the past
Brit had been convicted, sentenced to the pen, I was proud,

Protective of my Colony's good repute, and out to see it last,
So ordered Baily gone, decamped within three days, or else.
Replied that yes he'd served, behind the bars, but too by cast-

Ing votes, had held elective office in the Commonwealth,
Opposing there the rabbit-like increase of a Monster Bank. Took
The Law upon himself, tempted on a smaller scale

To do as the Second on a grander did. Turned a petty crook,
Fabricated bills, interest free, then paid in full.
Let out, had stolen away to this godforsaken place wherein it looked

To him he'd at last be left alone, not called upon to pull
Another's load. Had his crime behind, his solitary life ahead.
Ready to believe on hearing this, yet not to be a gull,

I rode to visit Brit, listened in delight to all he said,
Saw his farm progressing right along, and left him there
To find his peace. Know he has, dead and buried.

Is better off, seeing how our ways compare,
His hopes for keeping friends from wrack and ruin,
Usurious rates. In remembrance seem to wear

His very shoes, pinched by those I warned against
The agents sold them land on scrip, counterfeit
As Baily's bills, though none in the end so innocent.

& hearing you now have come again
to follow down each hall each river-street
intent on recovering those lives from then
through an accounting though incomplete

to trace at least the vividest & reinvest
in all you intended a place should mean
revealed through friends & those professed
the words & ways these lines would glean

Guadalupe

begin *in medias res*
with this artery given the name
of a town in New Spain took its own
from another the conquerers left behind
when they set their billowing sails
to rejuvenate the old by endless veins
ingots up the Indian anus    sneaked out
from royal shafts    brought to piles
down from mystic pyramids

was where her temple stood
protectoress of
the Totonacs
Tonantzin she
mild goddess of
their earth & corn
not human blood
but turtledoves
birds she bid them bring

even there where later came
the Mother of God
to a native of Cuatitlan
his appellation from Nahuatl
changed to Juan
at her command the roses gathered from
a barren hill of Tepeyac
turned to a dark blue maguey cloth
with stars about her imaged print

is here a thoroughfare to drive or walk
awake or in remembered dreams
by night in its azure light
by day beneath cerulean skies
far from his vision in that humid cell
her miracle hung from hut to cathedral
a guide for taxi or transit bus
Virgin still is giving birth
to the hopes of rich & poor

this a pavement bears that sensual sound
though one so mispronounced
or call it "The Drag"
to some perhaps    to others none
each corner to those an angle on
measures more than surveys made
to those can look & slowly gauge
where & when each picture show
each glass door or window opened

yet closed to those
with darker skins
could see no film
even Indian friends
would file then back & forth
with signs to let them in
cursed by every weekend crowd
cordoned by ushers heard a repeated phrase
"Do you sell tickets to every color & race?"

gave first & still gives now
welcome to the wandering mind
the hero home to wife & child
the wastrel's return from exotic points
where it all began & comes back true
a dream of renewal within the old
within the steady stream of those
once gathered & started here
a parade rejoined & marching to

incarnations one & all
of more than they could even know
beyond their own unspoken prayers
any hopes had dared to hold
kept secret from a deepest need
by getting ahead driven off the course
left high & dry by the push to arrive
till now at last to have their say
to find it even in a narrow way

will bring them back
to this city signed their lease
the one they had to break    to tack
in search of freedom's fleece
karats of computers & seismographs
only too late to discover it flat
had fallen from that earlier grace
a disillusioned crew blown here again
restored by this Aeolus memory bag

recounting those days on rented skates
wheelchairs run on rechargeable cells
bicycle moped shuttle & roller board
blind with dogs or tapped white sticks
the short brawny guy clicked his tongue
as a sonar sound bounced off the curb
would tell him when & where to step
for making his way along this street
better than any assumed so self-assured

this truest path the one abandoned
misled by the salary a degree held out
had to leave it to learn its truth
or stopped by Charlie's deadly aim
in a  close-up of such a tragic scene
the bloody part Fred Eckman's son
acted in a play of Greek invention
when here the mortal flesh & bone
brought home its distant meaning

to that very current stepped back in
a plugging of lives back into then
a Herakleitian change unstops the ears
a retake of that poet's class on Whitman
once more his marriage upon the rocks
a Scylla & Charybdis to Odysseus' ship
in '60 steering his way down this river-street
between thumb & finger a ligustrum sprig
replacing the lilac in Lincoln's elegiac lines

taught in that course on *Leaves of Grass*
would set this too    though only afterwards
had first gone east to the green glass shards
lured by a hospital road's contagious writing
only slowly back to the little known
an idyll from 1873 by Edward King
past 38th can still be taken in
with its "liveoaks near at hand" more "a temple"
than the "retreat of clouded reason"

made to see it first through Michael Evans'
"Mother Had Dementia Praecox Too"
printed then for '63 in *Triad* 2
"The hospital    I'd seen it
the old stone buildings crawling
with ivy    the vacant-eyed patients
spitting out between the bars
at passersby . . . you're a rebel
fighting something that's unfightable

. . . And that twisted poetry you write
. . . It's for your own good. . . .
. . . The iron doors . . . closed behind. . . ."
later the call one night from a man inside
committed by those fearing all he knew
saying his tale could make a mint
just bring a lawyer & a tape recorder
would reveal how high up the corruption went
of that part of his story never in doubt

said type it up    sell it to the media
they'll pay any price    whatever you ask
as for him release would be his only take
insisted    then made it please    then pleaded
to save him from the others wouldn't believe
it was all a mistake    he wasn't one of them
heard them trying to cut him off    to break in
get back away from here he began to shout
& after that the line went dead

cattycorner to the flower vendor's cornet tunes
serenaded bus loads on the edge lived under a bridge
the Stinky Lady's urine-stained polyester pants
Bicycle Annie's alpen pack & her aluminum crutch
smashed a driver's watch when he helped to lift
one of her secret-filled bags or her plastic sacks
a frantic rider found miles from an uptown stop
had left his winter jacket on that Capitol bench
felt its warm sleeves entered by another's arms

the Caveman slept under cliffs above Shoal Creek
said he ate trash & in five years was never sick
had picked it up too to keep this street litter free
in front of Saint Austin's offered crème de menthe
a half bottle of rosé gotten out back & one of vodka
in a garbage can came across a Bollingen Plato
claimed he had read all the hundred great books
Ariosto's *Orlando Furioso* his favorite poem
recommended love's lost tears in the moon-travel canto

boat people had survived & worked their way
to wash up on its far reaches north at Airport
three short winding blocks from Irma Drive
the Oriental Market run by the friendliest Thai
its shelves & aisles heavy with a seaweed smell
burned perhaps by a rival remembered him there
rebuilt & again was the neighborhood's single spot
to buy a blue Anytime or an orange Commuter card
on a check never bothered taking down the TDL

at 16th back to El Toro's where Hickey inhaled
wolfed down those enchiladas with cheese & chili
his description in *Riata* of buttered tortillas
even now the mouth waters at such chosen words
with Beeson had lived off their refried beans
George all set to say "hot plate" before the waiter
when he would come to serve the towel-held order
loved to catch the look on his brown-skinned face
so surprised so upstaged by his own simple phrase

& though a resident alien who for the first five years
grew ill from the lard & corn reek in any such meal
even María tried it & allowed it wasn't half bad
will cook from time to time in that El Toro style
yet still can't stomach questions perennial as weeds
"What kind of Mexican food do you eat in Chile?"
"And what do you have for Thanksgiving dinner?"
when from her lovely lips the debater's reply
"The Mayflower never made it south of the border"

to the Nighthawk from his room behind it on Whitis
George would go at 3 a.m. for his size-royal snack
Jim for orange juice freshly squeezed & half a stack
next door to the florist for *Riata*'s grosgrain ribbon
from the public library passed with Morton or Jon
with a bases loaded piano sonata recording of Ives
another pilgrimage taken with that solemn vow
fulfilled by creating from these façades & faces
a shrine to Estevan & all his going without

from Dacy's Campus Shoes' window displays
when in '65 penny loafers were all the rage
their lip-like slots kissing the shiny coppers
bright coins of sorority sisters all dressed alike
from there to Chile whose mines remain
the veins of a people still drained to pay
for bargains on sale in that Lebanese store
heard it sung in protest in damp Santiago
fitting their sexy feet in homesick dreams

his chaste & chastening nights yet unexpired
his darkened days still bringing to light
visions seen then & glimpsed again
in the flood of these go flashing by
swept up in this street's strong undertow
reborn on its miracles both new & old
by a Mexican town has remembered Spain's
all blended roiled within & interfused
to render him ever the homage he's due

who bought this future at his own expense
the few's fortunes amassed by his making do
in return sing the Co-op's "cattle crossing"
leather-lunged evangelist a Viet eggroll stand
these revisited along with Elisa's elementary
all the streets as in a row they ripple & weave
from east to west each flowing within his state
in the very order from Sabine to Rio Grande
as through this city bears his proper name

Sabine

that first semester here & as it should began
on this street furthest east in Waller's plan
where Andy had chosen the fanciest pad
shared with Gordon who ducked out early
for the old Music Building's recital hall
to practice on the organ reserved for then
or so he'd claim when his turn had come
to do the dishes    huge feet (*patudo* in Chile)
a mystery how he played one pedal at a time

but was needed to meet that higher rent
the apartment too expensive for only two
though Andy offered to pay the difference
could not believe that invasion at night
just as he screamed then leaped from his bed
when a sudden flash lit its one long room
certain he'd been struck by a lightning bolt
said rather he'd awakened & suddenly felt
one of the giant rats sitting right on his chest

unaffected by mouse traps set out for them
they would saunter off after eating the cheese
beat them with a broom off the garbage sacks
called the landlord said Just pinch their necks
but later brought over his steel-toothed claws
to catch them coming out through every hole
in that luxury apartment's limestone walls
would never've had them with cheaper rates
but remembered too for that promise made

on seeing an e.e. imitation in a display case
Bass's "o orange water lily" had won 1st place
in reaction the urge born to respond one day
how another's prize was to open the way
from that hall in Parlin to her Chilean face
later to follow in his steps at the HRC
in '79 as Jim Bagg's editorial assistant
saved from selling shoes with a PhD
starts given by Bob's win & the job he quit

his poem from *Corral* in that hallway exhibit
across from one with Eckman's double sonnet
both outside Mody Boatright's office door
Chairman of English when he would shuffle in
to his class taken then on the Age of Darwin
ash from his stogie ever flaking as it fell away
or chewed too short & soggy to light it again
his lecture on Hawthorne's prairie conflagration
indelible as a fire-resistant Bible's asbestos words

another on the social evolution of Graham Sumner
declared the struggle for survival a condition of man
poverty not to be abolished by the passing of laws
but by working each day that the weak grow strong
typed a term paper on Progress at that kitchen bar
while overhead the Neanderthals stomped & rolled
wobbled a rock wheel or some outsized mixing bowl
another mystery segues from this street to its river
in that freshman year to a trip taken while at Lamar

crossing it with Burkart's Brass Ensemble
for a performance at LSU in Baton Rouge
of the joyous piece Paul Holmes composed
in Beaumont in '58    born in Abilene in '23
studied theory here in the old music rooms
but a stone's throw away from Guadalupe
his pock-marked face    hands over-large
a man of gangly build & of a sallow skin
his notes so vibrant so warm & clear

such care he took to copy them out
each player's part in manuscript
with stems & rests a match in ink
for his sound so infectious & elegant
conveyed by every ringing phrase
his penmanship that even made
the tricky upbeat rhythms
his sudden acrobatic leaps
all somehow to come out right

the shock of discord never his way
reason enough he's rarely heard
would admit to liking Hindemith a bit
mostly fugues & sarabandes of J.S. Bach
never listened much to his fellow composers
feared drowning he said in the influence pool
Andy considered it a sinking not to swim
two guardian angels from then
each whispering a differing what to do

have heard the others & hear them still
their hows & whys of all these lines
any hope this poem may stay afloat
depending on each & every one
as much & maybe more on Estevan
his life & letters ever launching forth
where & when friends rented then
such lives & voices lifting forevermore
a writing would seek to keep them current

Holmes who wrote for harmony more
than any thought of fame or glory
& the same holds true for Estevan too
in '26 with things still touch & go
sent his warning to both bickering sides
to swallow pride & lay their arms aside
addressed his hard but friendly epistles
to the self-styled commandant had like himself
after tedious waiting won a grant to settle

*pero nada que ver con él*
this Edwards whose impudence brought
an outpouring of the public's protest
from those had long before he came
found a spot held greater promise
who had forded wives & kids & hogs
across this stream    their very Sabine
has named this redivivus river-street
living near Nacogdoches along this side

the Louisiana-U.S. line
its banks forever shaded by
dogwood sweetgum    red & white pine
announced he would send them back again
have every squatter bound in chains
his threats he bragged a hurricane
the Spaniards he branded an idle lot
stirred the Indians to join his band
to run those "foreigners" off

bribed their chieftains Mush & Bowl
declared their sacred burial grounds
a Republic where the free could reign
the Mexican government he shouted down
till in the end he & followers forced to flee
sent packing by their own red flags
their rhetoric of a thundering storm
hightailing it across the same Sabine
their typhoon tamed by Estevan's oil

his words to any listening ear
true music for all concerned
a concord heard along this street
in name records that time & place
when tempers ran a raging tempest
floodwaters of cacophonous cries
a drowning out all common sense
till calmed by the warm clear tones
of Estevan's admonishing prose

remind so of that composer's notes
his "Lento for Tuba and Piano"
a piece inspired by Robert LeBlanc
student switched from a lucrative career
as chemical or petroleum engineer
to an instrument awkward & slow
though with diaphragm under control
could hold his breath then boom it out
to pump to life Paul's song & dance

as Estevan too had held it in
his counsel kept but then released
in measured phrases render still
his advice so sound & soothing

"I would write directly
to the Governor of the State
Give him a full statement of facts
and a very minute history of the acts

Write in *English* and make an apology
for doing so    It is perhaps
a fortunate thing I have learned patience
in the hard School of an Empresario

for I assure you
that in this place
I have had full use
of all I possessed

Gaines and a few others
blamed Ahumada and me
for the course I advised
Fields and Hunter

are certainly killed
by the Cherokees
and all the other leaders
of his fanatic party

have escaped across the Sabine
and I advised a mild course
with those who were compromitted
in a secondary degree

Ahumada chose to pursue it
and for this a few blame me
but I have a consolation
worth more than the approbation of any

and the Mexican character stands higher now
than it ever did before   I hope the people of the Colony
will be satisfied for *theirs* is worth more to me
than all the world besides"

remembered it all through Holmes
his very music evoking Estevan
forgotten there in his foreign cell

in '22 had first come over
in dark as to his *Lively*'s fate
had left before he even knew

the company & its cargo landed safe
feared the Colony with
provisions seeds & implements

all were lost
those aboard that ship he bought
gone down in a coastal squall

had come ahead to secure for them
a settlement    a claim
to land for those

might never see the shore
might never speak their own again
nor even Spain's unfriendly tongue

seventeen there were
& Lovelace one
had loaned him toward the *Lively*'s cost

came not knowing what fortune would hold
in '56 a century later & even more
had come to meet with the Governor

in uniform here to represent
the Council's Neches troops
another river lived along

that photo still retain
taken at the shaking of
Allan Shivers' hand

wearing that brown Explorer tie
with Eagle badge & Beaumont sign
a print shows adolescent shining eyes

could not foresee the how nor why
of a whole life plotted here
as if Estevan had mapped it out

fallen upon by a Comanche band
took the little he had
then gave it back

all but the blankets
his bridle & mainly
his Spanish grammar

crossing the Medina into
the poorest land
he'd ever seen

a country vacant of everything
but prickly pear    to him
Laredo the site of perpetual drought

& indolence    traveling on from there
never once inspired
as Humboldt not so long before

hoped no other spot on earth
could prove so miserable as what he saw
between Monterrey & Mexico

a judgment shared by Berlandier
"a lover of solitude
and of picturesque views"

who found its "small
groves of huisache
—whose hairy fruits

make ink as good as gall—
the only ones which even slightly
interrupt the area's monotony"

encountered no herbaceous plants
but then the Frenchman notes
"despite the apparent barrenness

numerous herds graze nourished by
the thorny nopal
a wagon wheel broken on our first day out"

traveling there by car
could not compare
protected by tires from amygdaloids

earlier came here to play
a wayward erratic part
in Estevan's grandest scheme

his "seminary of learning"
though never dreamed it then
in that suit of forest green

the poorest excuse for a pioneer
planned to minister in any event
to pursue the course prescribed

by Reverend Birk
whose own began
at Jones Prairie & Walker's Creek

with boyhood idols of Buffalo Bill
& a threatened Texas Ranger had hidden there
out in the tall thick chapparal

drafted as chaplain to an island where
"The Purple Shaft" would plow into
those planes all parked & loaded

164 dead from 10 explosions
his own skull torn
when oxygen tanks

blew a concussion meant ever after
would stop the communion service
to stuff a *Kleenex* into his nose

done he said out of all respect
otherwise would suddenly drip
bright red in the silver plate

his last appointment to the church in Rusk
sent there by the Synod to recover from
a breakdown suffered at another charge

its famous hospital handy just in case
as pastor there served fewer souls
though still he'd forget his congregation

as his mind sped on
to a scene envisioned
at another frontier fort

its noonday sun glaring down upon
a dry parade grounds out of the past
inside their stockade a change of guard

when on the tip of an officer's sword
flashed the blinding eye of the Lord
contained & connected all time & space

wanted so to read as he    omnivorously
though too lazy ever to keep the pace
his devouring before he would move to another

every volume of any author's works
planned to attend    as he    Lon Morris first
then Southwestern above the San Gabriel banks

state's oldest university his alma mater
having heard like him that secret call
for a Methodist man of the cloth

or thinking then was intended to be
later recalled his sermon at evening worship
of a farmer stumbling behind his mule

who spied in the sky a big PC
took it as a sign to go Preach Christ
laid down his reins & answered

who after years of riding circuit
decided Plow Corn was all it meant
came rather to Poems Cast on this river-street

where Barker began Estevan's trip
never to enter nor enroll as planned
in the Perkins Seminary at SMU

Estevan's injunction so long unknown
the trail blazed by Moses overgrown
with believing had already passed beyond

any silly high school history course
one so filled with useless dates
the fiery cloud still up ahead

of pillars gone before
those would lend instruction
in a poetry struck from desert stone

though even Estevan missed the way
such lines may follow from
Berlandier's road to Monterrey

where huisache made
the writing flow
on looking back

retrace that route
another wrong turn has come out right
from Ciudad Victoria drove the Volks

through mountains never ending
the engine straining up one side
breaks whining down & around

winding curves where grinding trucks
hogged narrow roads hung miles above
each lush precipitous inviting plunge

each range revealing a higher yet
to reach at last that valley floor
its cacti where the Aztecs saw

their prophesy's snake
wriggle in an eagle's beak
& in spite of all as it did for him

that trying year of highs & lows
proved of lasting benefit
his own to those may never know

nor ever care how much it's worth
beyond any estimate or budget spent
his own limited funds all running dry

sold his watch for food & drink
for posting the latest news to his brother Jim
drawing on Hawkins to tide him over

then ran into an Englishman
loaned him a little more
that General on a mission for

the Chilean state
had fought against its Spanish rule
he an ambassador

perked up at Estevan's Texas plan
even agreeing to split with him
any grant should come his way

& just the same would Wavell
share whatever lands the Texan gained
Arthur Goodall

a guide well-versed in Latin life
his Spanish good
Estevan's improving day by day

wrote to the Congress as best he could
appealed they stay decentralized
not to keep as the Romans had

every province bound to Rome
not to make of its capital city
the nation's single seat & center

Wavell meanwhile reminiscing
of the audacious attack Lord Cochrane staged
his capture of the fortress at that southern port

Valdivia where Cortínez arranged
for the talk on Williams & Spain
in a Spanish even now no match for Estevan's

there met Carlos' dancer wife    later estranged
with Omar Lara his poet-communist friend
exiled in Rumania after Allende's fall

Gonzalo Millán in Montreal
Oscar Hahn of black rose fame
who came to this state

in '62 on the same
Chile-Texas exchange
in turn had gone there in '65

returning alone in '66
with María & Darío in '71
Hahn's generation read & followed

translating their lines & lives
vines & tendrils kept curling back
to their long thin envisioned land

a tree whose limbs
they would lop but love
as Hahn who in '73

fled to a salaried job
in Maryland & later the Iowa Workshop
that week with María in his own Arica

welcomed there by Oscar's colleagues
to lecture in that very same room
where shortly before Vargas Llosa

delivered they said a magisterial speech
though Hahn did not come out
to greet be seen with or hear

a Texan spoke so haltingly
Ramón Layera to end up here
with Jo & the kids exposed

to his trial by fire for tenure
rendering Harryette Mullen for Prickly Pear
before that had brought over Lawrence Benford

in Arica with Espagne Pauner
led calmly by both through thorny fields
of fists & objections the leftists raised

escorted too by Alicia & Oliver
on his radio show to be excused
for imperfect tense & faulty case

& yet by chance would use
a Chilean expression so dear to all
"to think oneself the death in boat"

got a laugh from their comic phrase
how many later to be herded aboard
sailed off to years of wistfulness

in Oliver's letters the disillusion
from party promises unfulfilled
though he & Alicia never played the part

the convenient role of refugees
from quote the C.I.A.'s overthrow
taking their lumps in Birmingham

to struggle through without complaint
in '71 a turn of events so unforeseen
though in '66 Carlos looked even then

to leave Valdivia's endless rain
its only other season/station the one for trains
its earth damp three hundred sixty-five days

where humid clothing hung to dry
before the oil or paraffin stove
smoked until the windows fogged

his books of Borges' poems
known from then
a friendship formed of all these years

starting off from where
Lord Cochrane had led his men
through cannon fired from high above

worked their way through timber & mud
up paths along those sheer rock cliffs
Carlos himself later under the gun

had left his wife & children behind
to come to scale in Iowan drifts
steep bulwarks of a terminal degree

to storm his way to victory
to win it in himself
the going tough

bogged down by dull demands
delayed by deep affections
pinned him down

the daily need
for love
escaped by none

the assault on a foreign front
an endless siege
then came to share

to walk this city's river-streets
as had with him where Cochrane won
his visit here a dream come true

to show Estevan's setting for
his wished-for language school
& what did he feel

when Wavell spoke
of Carlos'
Andean land

did he see his Colony gazing south
creating bonds as close as these
turning from a deep dependence on

the east with its hold like Rome's
know common views could bridge the gulf
establish a Mediterranean trade & art

hearing of his talk with that Englishman
now once again in memory climb
Santa Lucía      Santiago's Cerro

at the center      at the heart
of María's capital of her country too
to repeat the history of the Beauty kissed

held first where Pedro de Valdivia
battled the Araucano in epic form
his city founded upon

the eucalyptus-shaded lovers' hill
with its statue of Caupolicán his bow drawn
in that war ended for him as he sat upon

the Spaniard's sharpened pole
would break & gore his innards
with pain enough to weep & plead

yet met his death with no grimace
his face serene his eyebrows never twitching
in ecstasy as though on their wedding bed

till at his feet his Fresia threw
a son suckled at her own breasts
child of a captive father changed his sex

in shame to sever that sacred knot
Ercilla's past from María's lips
tasted ever after with each embrace

carried to catch & hold her fast
by this river-street goes through no more
by an apartment then so overpriced

went down before
the campus expansion's wrecking ball
two cities     two continents

now spliced as one
by a minor composer's major chords
an attuning to that empresario's fervent prose

links from Apennines to Andes
farms since Horace     a plantation near Bolivar
at St. Paul's a minister spread the gospel

his good word pointing the road to read
irked by a poem & stirred to reply
though none has ever quite satisfied

through the writing elected in '65
to that student leaders' *intercambio*
along with those like Ricardo Romo

track star-historian & on & on
through every hypocrisy
would stand between

her more than any hope or answer
all tying as Estevan's letters
Araucanian with Texan strands

no Graham Sumner's loose connection
but an Explorer's bowline strong as scripture
will never tangle nor ever slip

Red River

with its sandy land & ruddy undrinkable water
Altus a Texas town till they switched the border
from north to prairie dog of this river's forks
on either side salt cedars with wheat & sorghum
though living just across what a difference it made
longing each day for home & a place would swear
had crops superior to those any Okie could grow
caught sore throats from that air breathed in
picked up such narrow notions epoused ever since

how account for its creation of that Sooner hound
can never dispute nor forget his knowing look
his name chosen by mother when she volunteered
to take a rambunctious after-school Cub Scout den
he a part rat terrier would wear each badge in turn
wolf lion webelo (bear skipped with a change of age)
sewn on a leather patch & hung from his collar
on hikes waxpaper-wrapped for him his half-a-can
swam the Neches twice    more than earned his Eagle

survived Houston to whimper under a Beaumont bed
buried by his Hildebrandt Bayou he loved the best
a slough out near Humble Oil's refinery camp
where he had chased & barked & dug in holes
after brown swamp rabbits & armadillos
slowly lost his hearing then hit by a car
crawled home to that music room behind the garage
far from his birthplace where in those alien fields
locusts sing & shed on mesquites their empty shells

with mom & dad & Tommy returned
back across the south fork of this river line
to stay with Nan that first spring there
a week in Fort Worth to cure whatever ailed
always it's been the same outside this state
in Mexico once more such illness took its toll
María so delighted to speak her *lengua* again
bargaining in the shops & the open-air stalls
while was laid up for days by those smells alone

203

as Estevan languished in that dingy cell
with feverish dreams of pecan & liveoak
with fears his colonists would overreact
saw Butler with horns & a pointed tail
.misguiding them all to dissension & war
uncertain if letters were delivered or read
his patience tried if not beyond about as far
as ever a Ben Franklin or a Job endured
his prayer one last time to see Peach Point

to be with Mary & sit quietly in the shade
of sweetgum forming a canopy above
in a blend of holly & her sun-dried hair
their thoughts entwining as covering from
the political sun with its nightmare rays
to make it back home & the work to be done
to bring them together & better each one
or forget them & think of himself for a change
o best to recall the snail & its lowly pace

have a local mind from that inextricable time
uprooted at nine by dad's decision to move
to cross over & sell his Great American Life
to farmers would show the pulling of bolls
to drive the muddy roads & hook blue cat
bass with mouths could open big as a fist
then back across to visit with Alvin & Sis
on the way with Huck & Tom inside a cave
but from any moving car got nauseous sick

never making it through those classic books
for more than a dozen or fifteen years
not even here in '60 that spring semester
read instead Dickens' *Great Expectations*
Gogol & Dostoyevsky & some Latin to boot
sharing then that rat-infested luxurious room
on Sabine just up one block above Red River
where first Dave Reck & then later Jon Bracker
set down their notes & poems in shaded homes

at black or white repainted desks worried their way
to a 12-tone piece    one on drinking of light & dark
houses replaced by an asphalt sea with liveoak isles
lost for the sake of late models parked on tar
on weekends for the Longhorns' rabid followers
chanting as defenses shut down Hogs or Frogs
rarely missed a Mustang Bear or Cougar contest
yet want them back as a signal caller's errant pass
when on his last attempt a linebacker intercepts

on Frank Erwin's orders would remove antique elms
defied by students had themselves chained to them
despised that Regents Chair with half-lens frames
who killed too the exchange between Texas & Chile
Dean King was surprised to learn opera his passion
Ron the librarian mastered Italian hearing the Met
by a higher rise Erwin increased seating capacity
for six Saturdays a year sacked a summer's relief
from May to October their green protective leaves

for viewing artificial yards in a conference race
with Wally Pryor summing it up play by play
that feeling of a saving tackle a handoff taken
of gaining the first & ten on a third down five
on a quick-opener to pop through & break it
not turn the ball over on that final critical drive
to suck it up for a last-ditch come from behind
snag a sideline toss & tightwalk just in bounds
dance into the endzone as the clock runs down

the intricate formations marched at half-time
those patterns repeated for keeping in step
to memorized tunes practiced morning & night
to the letters & emblems & human designs
performed on a field with each other in mind
all as one to execute a sharp to the rear
to pivot for a diagonal on precisely the spot
a routine rehearsed & while put down as dull
held up an end belonged had a weight to pull

later on would prefer Rice's chaotic "Mob"
helter-skelter in their disorderly non-uniforms
darting every which way to avoid any semblance
then come together & spell an opponent's initials
to pay tribute in playing the rival's fight song
to the applause for making such fun of it all
always to include a social or political point
a current comment on a world gone wrong
while crowds consume nachos & popcorn

Darío earning himself some pocket money
selling sodas in stands to the thirsting fans
in between his practicing of Bach partitas
his exercises in math or in chemistry lab
to await his turn at the back of the line
his trays of *Cokes* toted to blasting bands
for the fraternity flasks of instant courage
disagree with Joe Jones of Waller Creek fame
would have trees sure but lessons too of athletics

Estevan's city for memories not these alone
destined as well for the others certain to come
even to "The Overlook" odious condominum
erected by "The Shiflet Group" ruined the view
from windows where in July's sweltering heat
could view the cool bamboo on Poplar Street
though one block long never remembered short
in thought from semesters there going on & on
unlike any student account stamped overdrawn

upon demand each matching garage apartment
paying the bearer in full from a formative day
with its arch at the foot of a wooden stairway
a set ascends the inner walls of all who are
fruitful though facing a bare treeless yard
still stuccoed white from that unrushed time
when few owned or could even afford a car
walking to classes & for the week's supplies
to sneak previews at the Paramount Sunday nights

*Peyton Place* or *Blood and* (wilted) *Roses*
back from town through the Capitol dome
by way of Elisabet Ney's the leading man
though his coming attractions untaken in
history then seeming less real than film
a girl's first kiss a vampire at her throat
set hearts to throb not agrarian thoughts
his lines from a letter dated Brasoria 1829
on nothing more than a harvest of crops

would meet Bracker there by accident
in his tiny room below & at the back
his package left in that upstairs box
took it down & knocked on his door
to be welcomed in to much of his life
to the green potatoes & a heating plate
his painting by Klapp of people eating
to long talks with him of Keats & Yeats
to hear with his friends a Brahms or Haydn

did *Penny Poems* at Amarillo & Wichita Falls
his cards & letters to arrive from Paris
Terre Haute New York & Slippery Rock
Hawaii Manila Singapore & San Francisco
in Japan a towering giant so ill at ease
with his prominent feet & oversized nose
wandering at sea carrying the extra baggage
of a sister unvisited a mother unwritten

the heaviest load a wife he'd given up on
stopped by without fail but never to tarry
replans once more to start fresh & settle
his poems can move in spite of constraints
to make them pleasant by prosodic rules
was there he painted his father's portrait
left with somebody or other somewhere
sketches scattered as so many leaves
in '61 sat still for him in his only chair
then grew so morose withdrew from school

but before that had had a falling out with George
& after he'd left went on rooming alone
found Jon a boon but everywhere inequity
dropped out & in despair showed up at home
then returned in June ready to try it again
to rent with Andy that other twin side
the eastern upstairs with Lloyd below
hefty blind student made his condition a joke
would spend his tuition on a trip to the coast

those carefree days when parents paid
for the learning more outside of classes
than in any courses had enrolled to take
appalled by failures & switching of majors
by rooms looked to them pig sties or worse
dirty clothes under beds or thrown in closets
weeks of unwashed dishes so fungus-caked
anguished to understand such finding of fault
with truths they'd acquired such harder ways

in '28 Andy's own folks Margaret & Paul
studying at what then was Texas Wesleyan
its director Reverend Olander Swedish too
in the college co-op both earning their keep
by doing such chores as milking of cows
their fees by cleaning the dormitory house
their teachers themselves University students
later they too attended & pursued their degrees
but with Depression quitting to make ends meet

she a maiden Anderson from nearby Manor
her father styled himself foremost an author
stole time from breadwinning to finish his text
writing it in a lively readable patriotic prose
on the pride in his being a *Hyphenated* man
an immigrant citizen linked to a newfound land
in love like Swante Palm with the printed word
that Sir collecting books of kooks like Darwin
neighbors howled when Anderson printed his own

Paul another second generation from over by Hutto
a little crossing there on the San Gabriel's wet fork
rose 3-miles wide & moved a plumbingless house
his blacksmith father told that story "and as it goes
when none could settle on a name for the town
one Swede spoke up & said 'I guess we gotta Jonah'
and it stuck"    regaling too with slow endless tales
of a sulphur plant put in in a Wyoming snowstorm
"well now you might say it weren't exactly no snap"

nor was it then to explain to a friend
or write the poem meant what was meant
much less locate the girl would last forever
ask Andy who thought for certain he had
a redhead from Lamesa would lead him on
& how many others to feel it wasn't worth it
when always the words just came out wrong
the native speakers so inspiring in Batts Hall
on exams their accents making no sense at all

in Latin had James Hitt & Christian Smith
can never get over having ever let go
of that dead language they offered alive
after the convolutions of Cicero to arrive
at *The Aeneid* abandoned after one canto
a voyage only known in verse translation
that ur-journey missed in Garrison Hall
with its wooden desks such tested ships
by passages ventured on that ancient sea

how Estevan would not have been pleased
but then he never had to stand there in line
march back & forth at the Varsity Theatre
in that movement had its beginning in '62
would integrate every off-campus movie
seemed harmless enough at the local "Y"
taking part in meetings held by the SDS
nailing picket signs at the Methodist Center
then holding them up to be taunted & jeered

by voices from the back of the passing bus
yelled they didn't need no white boys' help
as if getting even with him in a Mexican jail
had gone to further Moses' colonial dream
not hardly just spiting whoever they saw
unconcerned & unaware he had gotten off
even to figure it out later hard to swallow
could not then because had not even seen
the book where Barker has set it all down

knew only those rooms he had lectured in
Garrison where Hitt declined the declensions
or sat in the Old Library named for Eugene
preparing for classes that spring semester
with serial novels in pairs assigned by Cline
dumb taking Russians & Victorians together
fell asleep in those plush brown leather chairs
beneath high beams with their angles & stars
by lamps cast soft light on words & floors

reached by marble stairs splotched with gray
a stone in use below for those urinals too
the men's with its brown-stained wooden doors
its knifed & dated plea "Susan I need you"
& how did he expect her to find it there
even to have heard Estevan's biographer
would that have aided in making it through
to have had that teacher of history explain
how such crises have come & will again

or to have listened to him in Houston say
to that audience how "Recurrent doubts
are a wholesome antidote to complacency"
would that have made a difference then
when everything led to a pointless end
unlikely unless perhaps it had dawned
the very fact that his "Chief" Eugene
had a mind from Riverside & Palestine
though even Christian restored no faith

210

dropped Mister Enthusiasm's epic class
the truest of epithets for an Aeneas came
armed with anecdotes for all the fates
hiked & blocked at famed Temple High
an Entellus who put on Herculean gloves
his sense of humor a knockout punch
after a tennis match or leveling a house
will lift his flute with enormous hands
balance it at his lips to render an etude

but won't stand still for listening to Liszt
music of the unwashed with all their kitsch
rejects as Ez any usurious system of loans
has longed to erect a rammed-earth home
undaunted by a strikeout in the game of love
still a friend in deed to his three ex-spouses
does light or heavy repairs around their houses
on visits the kids sleeping crammed among
his Greek & Latin texts his Loeb classics

& had Estevan headed East can any have cared
for certain not those who criticized most
their constant resentment reason enough
to have left the reins in ungrateful laps
gone back & let them fend for themselves

always there are others to take one's place
can what any man does not be done by another
for suffering through where then is the honor
why bother when fault is found with the best
& in time a dozen at least may do it better

though none can deny the performance given
in success or failure the learning still earned
never to be taken away nor ever replaced
better than remaining unchanged & blameless
from fear too little or too much be said

the fiction student who for a solid hour argued
why be in *Bernie Feldman's Detective Cookbook*
said it would only be thrown in the trash
who never turned in a single assignment
to do or not to do the eternal clash

& if unfated it yet seems wholly needful
to descend in indecision to some nether world
& stumble there through each bubbling fosse
for the knowing all those have gone before
their works awaiting whoever would follow

when Webb too met with hopeless moments
would hold up the image of William E. Hinds
& think on the books his benefactor had sent
"However much I was tempted to quit
I could not quit without letting him down"

even before the first issue of *Riata* was out
an announced East-West theme came under attack
a discouraging satirical letter to the deadly *Texan*
gave new cause for thinking would give it all up
when resigning had meant no meeting with Jim

no trips to Red River & the Printing Division
to approve the plate & later to punch those holes
would show in the center of his blind embossing
a rice-paper endsheet with his burnt-orange smear
reviewed by Ambrose Gordon as a collector's item

never to discover Zanders' "Fugue for an Island"
John's story rejected by *New Campus Writing*
then accepted as edited with that change of title
in turn Jim hired by Printing as a book designer
if not for himself went on for Mary & Moses

but what to do with a disparaging Frantz
has seen Barker's *Life* as far too partial
or with Santa Anna's remark in Castañeda
how Estevan employed an English guile
to trick a generous Mexican nation

can contradict nothing answering the charge
had gathered the material as any despot would
had made a student's magazine too prettified
have chosen rather to re-remember that call
Come see Ransom at his Chancellor's Office

on his pile carpet before his mahogany desk
stood in awe & heard him say of that issue
reminded him of *The Quarterly* model for all
then on the editorial staff was offered a position
though funds as ever would never come through

as he spent instead his obscene figures
acquiring the works of the dead & buried
authors from Britain France anywhere but here
ignoring there on Rio Grande a Hickey at work
composing stories ungraced its expensive pages

ten years later left it for Hudspeth to run
even earlier had started its downhill slide
from halcyon days held Zukofsky & Dickey
with Kim Taylor illustrating their latest lines
then fell to a versifying of the safest type

in the Tower found Frances & her aerial view
chain smoking there in her masculine shoes
approached her naively to edit for free
return its past glory helping solicit the new
had no patience she said with the contemporary

blamed her alone for no poem getting in
María declaring it an obsession with print
lusting after another more bolder by-line
in Dante's age if not cardinal a venial sin
she they say kept academia out of the red

& after all the badmouthing thought & said
let in when Don Miguel requested a review
that omnibus coming out as "Who's Afraid
of the Big Bad Poem?" to feel an absolute fool
yet not at Ransom's behest so never the same

though later on when Bass would up & resign
leave Harry's "center of our cultural compass"
Ransom fulfilled his word in a roundabout way
through revelations gained in on-the-job training
from letters & photos his hoarding had saved

at Dacy's Congress St. store next to Woolworth's
never minded running fill-ins to that dusty stock
yet rather than shelving those slings & pumps
could take down from PRs a blue-covered *Ulysses*
in PQs Emerson's trenchant thoughts on Alighieri

through excerpts quoted in Harry's own essays
follow immigrant marks notched not on firearms
but in journal jottings by doctors & bookworms
Swante Palm Ashbel Smith & Sherman Goodwin:
self-examination is "duty insurance" to counter sin

though indebted again & again too late to repay
still enter in the account HR's bringing together
of the priceless proofs & manuscript drafts
an Estevan acting on each stranger's behalf
two magnets drew the plowmen & scholars

risking wreckage for the other's millennium
two men among many worked forever apart
yet joined in the mind as this river's two forks
with their cargo of hopes & rewritten dreams
for those to profit from their prophetic force

San Jacinto


down steps at Memorial Museum's western side
Proctor's sculpted rearing mustangs symbolize
"seas of pristine grass    men riding free"
unreined by the ruinous costs of oil & gas
once bore on their bare or saddled backs

explorers braves & cowhands plunged ahead
on Estevan's map of '29 whole herds fill up
his vacant tracks before the searing brands
of excessive horse sense broke their spirits
gone with the trails to Alberta & Cheyenne

while a block south in Memorial Stadium
Longhorns dig in for a goal-line stand
showing what it takes to come from behind
prove on another crisp autumn afternoon
how on being down one can turn it around

always this street conjuring that historic place
where at siesta time between the silken sheets
Yellow Rose would give herself for a 36th state
Sam surprising his tented "Napoleon of the West"
then opposed Austin as governor & capital seat

yet none of this has mattered to Joseph Jones
the vituperative troll on his noonday rounds
who's picked from his water unsightly plastic
attacking through inventories in poetic prose
those have cast it from sidewalk or bridge

for this city's drainage says more to him
than any points scored at a championship
& the only battle he's found worthy to fit
none ever pitched at a bayou-headed river
rather the struggle to save his campus crick

riffles beside shuttle bus & faculty traffic
as street & its stream meander together
from museum & stadium to Santa Rita's rig
then part as one flows on to Centennial Park
by the Drum & along to the Hamilton home

the other continuing toward Scholz's Garten
past pink office buildings of polished granite
the State Library with its anonymous portrait
of mild Estevan in oil on window-shade canvas
to 5th where Service set Joe's *Life on Waller*

his chapters written on near half-a-century
of sack-lunching to delicate or raucous calls
from purling creek's to wading grackle's
observing the ghostly crawfish scuttle
to gather in the high-carat sunfish gold

counting his riches in the moss's green
as it clings to a slab of fossilized stone
finding it in the cypress's fallen finery
patterns dropped unseen by pecan & oak
their patchwork sewing of light & shadow

came here first in '60 that spring semester
to read in the middle of Joseph's stream
*Vanity Fair* & alternately *War & Peace*
stretched at length on smooth limestone
its soothing eddying about & beneath

confused as to who was in which ballroom
by their uninvented wars so all the same
unaware of "an old codger" waged his own
against the University's landscaping machine
would narrow its banks & pour concrete upon

its water-carved bed    even bulldoze its figs
while those came back as Bobby Layne did
other sylvan ancestors never seen again
such luscious trunks cut down & any to come
the subject of the troll's outraged lament

his infernal fight making such total sense
his defense of even the lowliest weed
lobbied to make his creek a garden park
with two gauging-stations its record complete
a unique model for the nation to monitor

fearing for his city named Waterloo first
that with dumping of refuse it suffer defeat
a building blitz overrun its weak position
at the hands of careless mindless planners
neo-Bonapartes mapping outlandish growth

but how ban trashers from Estevan's heaven
generations brought up among cactus & sand
Elisa from joining in the Tchaikovskian dance
not 1812 cannon but Nutcracker's yule ballet
at the PAC within earshot of Jessen Cascade

where among the string section Darío played
the Brandenburg 6th & Musorgski's Mountain
María searching authority files at Public Affairs
& at the HRC raised out of turbulence & haste
allowed at last to make use of that final degree

bend ever towards somehow having them both
as live wisteria twining around the metal posts
beneath statued mustang band at Joseph's creek
with pungent clusters draped like bluish grapes
blooms through a demotic enrollment stampede

back then a low GRE would have meant the end
had it not been for insisting for near half an hour
to be given a chance by Hughes the acting Dean
to be placed on probation & be allowed to prove
was not   he said   material for graduate school

seated in his office on that forbidding first floor
with Barker's Library above it in Battle Hall
wasn't about to accept a raven's nevermore
had denied access to Estevan's archival bequest
to editing of *Riata*   being chosen for Chile

217

to find Beauty there at her binational center
another unsecured loan would make it all happen
taken out thanks to Lomax & his Ex-Students
later to return to fragrant Batts never forgotten
on forming a part of that professorial "pool"

each semester just before or after classes began
to have a low-paid temporary contract renewed
a fortune after having been in '64 barely let in
back in '76 teaching & to give the assignment
they compose poems seated beside its stream

to walk out of Parlin & across East Mall
toward the bridge back of Etter's alumni center
where John Lang Sinclair's pepsong yet hangs
its brown wrapping paper in his faded hand
to pass with that class the site of old B Hall

gone before that '61 summer saw movies shown
then in '62 on grass by Waggener watching them too
not to cram for the Arab Nationalism final exam
past labs of E.P. Schoch founded Longhorn bands
by ROT-C's flag to descend the fountain stairs

through windblown spray off its jetted waters
spill transparent in full view of B. Iden's Theatre
named for Payne told Ray who took his course
rooming then with Andy    how Olivier's eyes
always appear dead    see it most in his *Hamlet*

Andy himself into the classical *Symphony in C*
Igor's *Rake's Progress* set to Auden's libretto
in *Fantasticks* longest running off-broadway show
that Professor parodied by Tom Jones lovingly
former student learned from him as Rip Torn did

in '67 saw him in *Beach Red* with Cornel Wilde
another bloody war film on another Pacific isle
till the Japs    a father & son    turn suddenly real
snipers among infested jungles fighting with fear
marine invaders righteous as they stalk & kill

in that same Hobbs movie saw industrial waste
emptied on the screen to stain the river pink
*Pretty Poison* with Perkins disturbed at his best
pictures in that oil town only a handful attended
María beginning her labor there in a *Volpone* scene

brings back that walk down fountain steps
to this turnaround bridge & along these banks
to sit with Arnie Cheryl Peggy Jules & Gene
with their writing class to watch & listen
to compose with them from whatever came

a piece on Wukasch mover of Symphony Square
Darío playing on its stage by the rippling creek
between his trio & the audience on arena grass
while just across the stream on another occasion
lunched with Joe & Lord Byron his gimpy friend

watched as he hobbled but with beak held high
in spite of lameness claiming territorial rights
his feeder with khaki cap & a bag with straps
for collecting the discarded new & old artifacts
his glasses agleam with Waller's reflected light

clambered with him over knobby-kneed cypress
crawling under around through vines & willows
as he inveighed against racket of cars & mowers
needless motors    men mad for bronzed Bevos
had read Neruda's poem seated on Incan stones

professor began in '44 *The Library Chronicle*
taken up by Oscar Maurer    that veritable savior
could not have followed them at Ransom's Center
as trimmer of Turner's quarterly display window
treasures shown through it in Caledonia & color

the Brits & Frogs all so suddenly incensed
after laughing their ways to the savings & loan
from scraps deposited in this B-Western desert
unmindful of Rosetta stone & Elgin marble
to find with heritages GTT the joke on them

219

resented it with taxes siphoned so far away
leaving nothing here for those alive & active
no interest in this city's own books & prints
or so it seemed & even now can still appear
yet detracts little from the satisfaction taken

working with scholars who wrote from abroad
posting their articles or with a local like Slate
unraveled the screenplay by Zuk & Reisman
*Ulysses* from '32 with Louis 5 years into *A*
Joe weaving it like night without any quotes

in '77 had sent that class with Ted the cellist
to hear the Mahler 5th performed & describe it
had then as a teaching assistant Clare Colquitt
in '84 printed her piece on the *Contempo* years
another in '85 on Wharton's letters to *cher ami*

at Duke had met & married her Bradford
who would come as well to submit & please
with work on Sarah Coleridge's Spanish & Greek
on her editing of her father's impossible texts
her bout with the family's poppy disease

Irene Rostagno on Knopf & its Latin boom
Carpentier's *Lost Steps* Donoso's *Obscene Bird*
novels & stories from Amazonian backlands
tracing them all through the files & reviews
ins & outs of the career of Alfred & Blanche

Lawn on Russell's *Jazz Style in Kansas City*
Ross's Dial contracts with Charlie & Schönberg
Rick coaxing bassist Ramey out of retirement
born in '13 beside Waller at Red River & 14th
in on the birth of bebop with Parker & Monk

or exploring dark passages of letters to Dahlberg
slogging through those "squalid marshes of wrath"
by "dungy sheepcotes" bitten by the fleas of Sodom
Christensen unearthing Olson's "song of the Worms"
then reached a "dreary impasse" as bottom-dog friends

his lines emanating from Bryan as émigré Aggie
promoting Texas poetry through his radio tapes
featuring so many from McDonald to Burford
or a beat Gary Snyder a Black Mountain Creeley
in differing another chorus of Charles & Edward

in '81 put together that *Cow's Skull* collection
charged with bias & branded a provincial elitist
for excluding Paul when others weren't native either
leaving him out of a bilingual anthology of poems
when some had done little not nearly so much

Estevan preferring families to unmarried men
discouraged riff-raff not industrious debtors
where else go for working off farms had failed
harvest & roundup for long-suffering not drifters
neither first-come first-served nor room for all

King denied tenure with three books to his credit
his essays better written than his enemies admit
on Ezra's library     his triangle with Hilda & Bill
Michael's rich digs for others in the Ransom "theft"
his too gave release from tedium of making a living

& with Tom Zigal to have the privilege conferred
of catching & marking typos in galleys & proofs
checking the bluelines correcting head or footnote
regional surveys contributed to his *Pawn Review*
meeting with Luis to discuss *La calavera* & Perú

been deprived of John Sunder's Bancroft & Catlin
Cabeza de Vaca     a vital past encountered in them
on Prescott Webb's bobwired & windmilled plains
where Black cowboys & dogfaces reopen the range
where though Newcomb's aborigines driven extinct

they survive once more on diets of larvae & feces
corn & communal hunting & running down deer
from Ice Age to the white man's colder coming
with Kirkland & Petri as his warm exceptions
W.W.'s books on those artists' brushes & pens

that pencil & watercolor Randall repaired
with the aid of Conservation's fabulous lab
so vicarious so vivid in a way only Petri had
with a black boy on horseback turning to look
at the keg of water pulled as a white boy rides

as he holds in his one hand a wooden bucket
passing into the cacti from moss-hung trees
in the background a bonneted mounted figure
racing away at breakneck speed    at the rear
a black woman on foot    on her head a basket

Indian rock art painted in a Hueco Tanks cave
Dallas draftsman traced Mescalero pictographs
symbols Forrest redrew & saved from graffiti
Newcomb again to revive & have them printed
from his pages to Inshallah home of Jim Smith

at Waller & 43rd its tradition as host to the arts
marked by arrowheads from those sacred camps
Elisa invited to shine there at her first cast party
from Comanche flints to a daughter in leotards
to the early roles played by Bugbee & Barker

said he didn't know why he'd even bother
but go on over & have a chat with Dr. Crow
would do no good    said he could only agree
next-door to Parlin after that graduate advisor
but informed at the office that he wasn't there

sent off to speak with his assistant instead
being greeted at the knock by a billygoat voice
its gruff Come in called through opaque glass
& at his desk Maurer rarely lifting his head
peering into a drawer he would open & close

on hearing of Hughes & then of Crow not in
looked hard at the drawer & closed it again
in that pause would spot on one of his walls
the copy of a print by Jon Bracker's friend
Frank Stack's etching of a garage apartment

spoke of that & of Bracker first met in '60
Edited in its heyday *The Ranger* & how is he
from there moved on perhaps to bring up jazz
his favorites by far James P. Johnson & Fats
another Waller than the one paraphrased by Ez

through digressions intriguing as his Trollope's
he glared at his hands as they pushed & pulled
then came at last to ask though not looking up
what was needed & on hearing a permit to enter
jotted down & given    with his face still awry

on the other's to catch surprise & displeasure
as he stared at that note with Oscar's okay
a victory impossible with cut-offs & quotas
with rents beyond a lower middle-class means
& moreso with at best the grades just average

to have missed it all by an unacceptable score
yet must confess he never slammed the door
though then & there thought it hardly a crack
over the long haul would open the floodgates
as it delivered this store of rivers & streets

the verses & visions in those houses & halls
meditations on Waller where Joseph patroled
finding him alone there still clearing debris
of fallen trees & sewage so backing it up
into foul gray stands of polluted scum

while on committees colleagues maneuver
to dam the way for some grant or raise
to fire the instructors have carried the load
or those like King had proven their worth
while a full professor rummages in disposal bins

his briefcase filled with smashed aluminum cans
not so much to recycle as to augment his pay
another in nifty tennis togs & matching shoes
ever ready during office hours for a set or two
Joseph at Waller on weekends or only at noon

cleaning the creek that it move & glisten
to preserve its creatures for future viewers
in its seasons to read literatures here & afar
lecture on World English till the mandatory age
though eager still to learn its language of flow

so how keep them back from his finest teacher
with pupils like Heraclitus Walton & Thoreau
let another old codger come if only just one
for it takes but a single life versus the litter
to proffer to the current its lessons live on

one able to draw from its deeps & shallows
a slaking drink of near or distant cultures
can take its history as a rod to measure
the insatiable will to fuel & horsepower
another steward of the wisdom in water

San Antonio


at 21st
with the playground empty
with its wire gates open wide
have crossed the asphalt often
where during their hour outside
her classes dodged or shot the ball

at not much more than 4-foot tall
here where she taught at Saint Austin's
in the Paulist fathers' parochial school
was towered over
by the 5th- & 6th-grade boys
though in the little she wrote never came up short

at Goliad
the superior marksmen
were surrounded & caught
in an open field
surrendered their arms
with cover & food in nearby woods

at twenty-seven in '74
mysteriously dead in Ecuador
disappearing in Guayaquil
weeks later washed ashore
the beach where she had walked alone
repeating new poems shall never hear

at sight of their games
think first of her
& then of all this city's lost
her lines like bars of gold
in a sunken galleon off the coast
no salvage crew will ever float

at the mercy of artillery pieces
gave their carbines up for dreams
of arriving back across the Sabine

both wounded & whole of return
all of a joyous reunion
with wife & children

at her going knew
more than most
of the naked heart & soul
of "what remains
when one is stripped
of all accoutrements"

at even her height & age
saw above all else
her body's one sharp tool
her artist's tongue
has spoken upon
"Is not Was nor Will Be"

at thirty Fannin
still brash from resounding defeat
of the enemy his troops sent reeling
though by them outnumbered 60 to 1
was ordered to invade & then to retreat
in vacillation branded a cowardly traitor

at the moment of love
she describes a descending
to the kingdoms of
animal mineral & plant
"all we once were"
& "whence we come"

at his erectile pointing she views
in four directions feels & pictures
the two of them "one wonderful well-oiled
machine" herself the "Borealis all afire"
not knowing where his compass ends
her magnetic north begins

at Urrea's hands
clemency had seemed assured
yet Santa Anna unconvinced
instructing instead that most be marched
along the upper & lower fords
be lined up there for slaughter

at a loss to say
how high a pint-sized
Susan Lucas    no gusher she
in living longer
might have reached
could hardly hazard a guess

at this corner with its kicks
& yells of recess
can only recall her distant walk
low & unaccommodated as nuncle Lear
yet even with less of her bullion left
outgrades any player twice as tall

at the commotion & smoke
28 escaping among the mesquite
drifting down the river names this street
far from a fate she's come to share
by an intersecting of poems & heroes
with those remembered 300 & more

## Nueces

was this the street where Donnie stayed
favorite of granny Polk on daddy's side
who dropped his date off near Forest Park
slid on a wet curve lost control & died
Tommy after delivering his Green Berets
flipped & crushed under his steering wheel
that cousin first & then that only brother

such losses still remote on arriving in '54
only later would find this city a sanctuary
one flown to year-round by migrating minds
seek a climate more conducive to ideas & art
found Donnie's fraternity in mourning then
for a member died in a wreck the night before
the wake on Lavaca at the Scottish Rite

its windowless walls as mysterious as death
walked past them then from town to campus
on that first trip here by Greyhound bus
a representative for Scout Week in February
put up at Bergstrom in the Air Base barracks
attended a Union ball where Sinclair's "Eyes"
yet peer across West Mall to Architecture

stood looking on as the cute couples danced
thrilled to be a part though ever at a distance
if future times & friends then dimly perceived
felt somehow nonetheless this city's heartbeat
the wonder of those Commons looming ahead
to gather there for hearing with Hickey's circle
his pronouncements so outrageous so subtle

in '62 Franklin Haar's poems stained & smudged
typed with inkless ribbons on those coffeed sheets
remodeled in '77 caught phrases for *The Poet Trap*
"heavy with Hamburger fog" "rehearsals downbeats"
when Laura & Renee listened to that brass quintet
played where Shirley Bird Perry had Jesson engrave
emblems in limestone above an expanded entrance

to those of longhorn mocker cactus & jack
horned-frog an owl a prairie-dog a rattler
added rook & knight comic & tragic masks
harp & lute along with quill brush & palette
festive grapes an opened text a swaying nude
all embraced among learning's leaves & fruit
but then it may not have even been Nueces

& yet that first day so distinctly comes in
to Webb his clear as "pictures on a screen"
though set to record 3 unforgettable precepts
left on his typewritten page a blank unfilled
now locate two vacant lots two blocks apart
one for certain right where Walter first lived
when from the MK&T took a streetcar north

on the other a frat house the city condemned
razed in recent years after its members hazed
a passing student kicked & pissed on him
would this have been that cousin's then
Webb as a frosh in on a sophomore's shooting
a fight in '12 brought passage of the hazing law
but failed to save a Corps cadet dead in '84

each on a corner    the Greeks' at 24th
Walter's at 22nd    such worlds apart
the former's brick now reduced to rubble
but thanks to all John Morris's trouble
the latter transported to a garbage heap
where goats had grazed on native grass
its windows in view of Balcones Fault

whose if not of each & all
have failed to read or ever to right
past or present for the future's sake
will leave it for a John to sacrifice
that all may know where Webb first wrote
recall how across & down this street
Bugbee came to rescue Estevan's repute

its panels of a history of tongue & groove
of "pumpkin" pine made tung-oil smooth
porcelain knobs on doors of a perfect fit
in '80 before Webb would room & board
kids by height scribbling their arithmetic
on Miss M.V. Jones's Select School walls
early solutions for any would double-check

each recovered by John's detective love
for Pompee's fine hand-slotted frame
that wheelwright's 1875 German-French design
remodeled & added to circa 1880 or '79
to preserve it John losing wife & daughter
Anne preferring IBM & the corporate gains
ex-spouse of her first taught a bit of Russian

would lead to shores of Pushkin's poem
his bronze horseman's stately Neva
grown restless with wind & a backing sea
tossed & turned as a bedridden invalid
till it rose & drove its wedge of water
between Yevgeny & his dearly beloved
John's restoration became a Nueces in flood

such pain of separation relieved by spraying
his Wright's pavonia    an endangered species
watching his garden stones darken with wet
bacon & alibates flint for lightening the day
jasper chalcedony dogtooth calcite crystals
copper cedar roots strips of petrified wood
varieties of cactus experts all on survival

his own spirits lifted in dampening these
observing his lichen thrive in their colonies
the patient decades they had taken to build
their green encampments on the barren fields
plowed under by developers in an afternoon
those would profit from a John's seclusion
forcing another move of his matrimonial home

the odyssey of a house where Webb composed
country boy wrought up by the magic meaning
of words set down in their orderly rhythm
with a music for those now & those to come
though a writing course he'd not recommend
just wide-reading bridgebuilding hoboing poker
well-drilling lovemaking windjamming war

John a model in that historian's mold
reared on the range up near Amarillo
from here to Houston drove a moving van
like Terry Raines the native printer
had done it himself whatever it was
John's Russian major "oh it's nothing much"
Terry of his geodesic dome "anyone could've"

their unassuming manners so sickening
how ever hope to master English even
any mechanical failure can hardly fix
these salvage repair restore resurrect
Terry's outside stairs of scrap rewelded
joists from a demolished university roof
Seton iron    born himself in Brackenridge

both granting to those a second chance
an elevator door given to rise again
rejected pillars to support once more
Terry exploring Texan & Mexican caves
the cool of his own deep modest ways
John renewing underneath the veneer
his house's date    its truest colors

Terry's bunk & woodstoved cabin
constructed in a stand of oak & cedar
just off the Kyle to Wimberley road
with on one side a grassy arroyo bed
facing a tree-topped limestone ledge
left its bathroom without any door
opened to creek & passing deer

from a telephone pole & lumber
built it first with its lighted path
leading to where the print shop's now
to a pond dammed up & rocked about
stocked with ducks & sodded around
from a sturdy trunk ran a cable down
to sweat then slide from slope to splash

had only begun just beyond the rise
a two-storey house of his own design
the shell of his & his Suzy's home
living meanwhile atop the circular shop
in a windowed room overlooks the grove
its leaves & tones in their coming & going
he at sundown reading or at the piano

in work boots in his plaid flannel shirt
his cap on above his sun-tanned face
with nicked glued & ink-stained hands
playing Bach inventions on a baby grand
in between his Heidelberg two-color runs
burning the plates for an overdue job
collating & binding & trimming it out

would exasperate so with constant delays
Jim at midnight doing the dummy again
re-moving the head & re-spacing a line
would wait on both with a shortened fuse
shoot off then feel the remorseful recoil
knowing this pair made the poetry go
a layout & printing to match the muse

all three to do it having paid the price
or kids & ex-wives have borne the cost
a son ever uncertain to which should turn
for years never touching nutricious food
would eat no vegetable no fruit no salad
dropped out from public & private schools
tried this tried that friendless confused

with fresh spring or cool fall mornings
born before the cabin or the ovaled bedroom
daughters awaked to a stranger slept over
to mothers cooking meals in a rusting bus
still parked within sight of a latest live-in
summers split between the parental dreams
immolated on altars of idyllic communes

though Bugbee & Estevan knew none of this
instead of marital the misery of Fort Bliss
never to tie the knot would stick to their books
to balance the accounts & write them all down
for those hereafter should inherit the land
or those later on would long to discover
who tilled it first who ran with the ball

Lester's flyer covered with Rootatorial cheers
the ads cut out & all the newspaper clippings
of a Longhorn game when by clever dodging
the 'Varsity boys laid it on Houston's ten
knocking their whole line into smithereens
with Bethea scoring behind that Texas wall
though "Wortham failed on every easy goal"

& when the fullback sang in the U's Quartette
Lester retaining as well that sheet music part
the program including violin & mandolin trio
as gowns cooperated with the citizens of town
a Hancock Opera House *Ben-Hur* performance
photos collected of Whitman at ages 53 & 68
of Gladstone too gave Lester his middle name

recording even Dr. Dayton's doggerel song
"The first of the villains who came to this state
Was runaway Stephen F. Austin the great"
some tarred & feathered in that leader's absence
by his friends' good intentions made deeply sad
of his Colony's first two years Lester noting
it had but one theft not a single homicide

mostly preserved the amount his subject asked
for the services to those were in want of cash
would receive any property not "a dead loss"
horses mules cattle furs peltry beeswax hogs
dressed deer skins or homemade cloth
"will sacrifice my own interest rather
than distress them for one red cent"

out of his own pocket paying a draughtsman
to plot the tract each deed called for
"The great expenses voluntarily incurred
must forever free him from the charge
sounds like sarcasm to speak of defrauding
'shook off the Yoke and dispersed the cloud
had so long kept his settlers in the dark'"

"Bugbee from even slenderer means
advanced money for labor and postage
to solicit *Quarterly* members by mail"
"grew to manhood in Johnson County
the post oak & black jacks of Cross Timbers
on the southwest fringed by the Brazos River"
"1890-91 lived at 2110 August Street now Nueces"

only "avoidable expense" his occasional trip
to visit the theatre to catch a Salvini
an Irving Terry in *Merchant of Venice*
the family concerned he had joined a fraternity
his mother sending extra money now & again
never telling the father who was so far in debt
"made 18 bales but won't come out much ahead"

like Webb went off later for the advanced degree
Walter never wanting to leave & said he believed
to have stayed in state had been much better off
a silly superstition to him this going away
said Oxford & Cambridge great from being inbred
on the train home after he had flunked his doctoral
luxuriated in a soft Texas voice's welcome drawl

at Columbia Bugbee working his way with ease
through the details massed to impede
but physicians' bills & the chronic school fees
his dear mother's death & his efforts to lessen
his sister's monotonous days back on the farm
forced his return before he had made it through
here to a pitiful salary with his time running out

always his classes prepared with exhaustive care
would never lecture but move from desk to desk
questioning & discussing each student response
after the bell all to gather about him for more
taking precious minutes from his unfinished Life
one recalled his winding & unwinding the chain
of a watch went ticking relentlessly amain

"In looking back I know now that over
and over again Bugbee's sound judgment
his knowledge of human nature     his patient
and persistent insistence
that young men may be led
but not driven
saved from disaster the B Hall experiment"

his allotment of a mere six active years
ending as the century turned to nineteen-one
in Woodbury near Hillsboro his studies begun
had taken part there in various debates: Resolved
that woman has more influence over man than money
"walked to Pleasant Point for the mail and received
a searching letter from DAISY declaring our friendship over"

That the white man has a better right to the States
than the Indian     That works of art are more attractive
to the eye than nature     at Mansfield College
wrote "Queer Queries":     What is the "River of Blood"?
Ans. Colorado: — signifying "bloody water"
from Horace copied how none's content with his own occupation
yet no one will exchange positions with another

235

entered the University January 1887
family resources stretched for the second semester
"along the line took an introductory course in the language
he was to use most in his subsequent investigations"
Spanish discouraged in the '60s the choice French or German
said no important literature written in it since Cervantes
but for February '65 discovered in *Motive* antipoems by Parra

a vein opened up in that Undergraduate's periodicals room
another lodestone would draw towards what richness to come
at Main under classical quotations symboled rafters at Barker
to read the lines & stanzas there & to take passage once more
to sink in seats & to hear those strikes still ringing true
moments placed in settings let them happen over & over
secret mine shafts how revealed     when & where the clue

pulled later to Ercilla Neruda Mistral & Lihn
Federico Blest Gana     Pezoa Véliz     Huidobro
to Cuba & the trapped tigers of Cabrera Infante
Macondo in García Márquez     Lezama Lima's paradiso
Carpentier's enlightenment     Rulfo Pacheco & Paz
the Tiresias affair in Borges     Sábato Puig & Cortázar
to the Marios' Montevideo     a green house in Perú

in San Felipe Estevan establishing first
instruction in English but of prime importance
the teaching of other of the modern tongues
"and especially of Spanish"     from a cholera attack
never fully to recover     gone by the end of '36
writing in March '35 under clouds of war
told Perry to "keep the children in school"

debunked by John Henry Faulk on public TV
as first real estate agent offered the others' lands
on lowest terms     Estevan's demeanor taking on
as the world turns a look so sinister & cubist
his crosseyed view of the darker as a barbaric race
"the enemy prepared to enlist the Negroes free or slave"
a serious threat to the white man's peerless civilization

statements made as his health & patience gave way
to Faulk just another enterprising racist
his passport to a promised land stamped nil & void
more a Moses forbidden entrance than his father before
reduced to a writer of ads & clever commercials
adept at attracting & luring the high tech biz
of today's Silicon Valleys & MCIs

in defense think quickly of John Seals in '60
linebacker & offensive guard ran wind sprints
with a fractured fibula    a philosophy major
on the '58 team the first recruited by Royal
now pediatric neurologist reads Johnson & Blake
only wore his jersey to that Plan II class of Silber's
knowing full well that Dean so abhorred the sport

Bugbee a booster both of the jocks & poets
a close associate of Ed Blount & Hans Hertzberg
the two "completely Bohemian in taste and conduct"
Blount later a dermatologist never happy he said
except in some dream-world creating his poems
French imitations or based them on Grecian stones
filled with nightingales he had never seen once

taken from most anywhere but his Hillsboro home
never from this city    not even the U.'s Forty Acres
from his passing train the closest an Arkansas scene
Bugbee sending their verses away to publishing firms
in between giving in History I & II the exams each term
"After 350 A.D. to what provincial official would an order
to organize an expedition against the Picts be addressed?"

Hertzberg's "Would-Be Epic" *Lawyers and Laurels*
printed here in '91 by Eugene Von Boeckmann
Hans' "Didactic History of the Junior Law Class"
more the sort of thing Bugbee must have wanted to read
who wrote for young men & women not to by-pass
their own University for some college out of state
"From every point of view this is undesirable

prevents the youths from becoming thoroughly imbued
with ideals obtaining" in their own backyards
"becoming thoroughly acquainted with resources
interests and the people of their own community"
must've cherished Hertzberg's use of a town or city
a native place name for each classmate's special quality
"young oak from Oakland" "a pine tall Tyler son of toil"

"Smith of Fort Worth fond of Tennis & Tennyson
makes much of racket & ball
but's sometimes silent in the Junior Hall"
those who towed the law & toed the waltz equally
"may they cut in life's quadrilles capers gracefully"
the short of stature but stentorian tongued
those came in lowest then finished on the highest rung

"Thro' meadows brooks in placid clearness flow
Without wild roaring or tempestuous show
So does our Junior Brooks' balanced brain
Work steady on
And 'shyster lawyer' will never soil his name"
of himself the poet will only say "am not thus vain
As to speak self while better men remain

The harpstrings break in twain—
Ne'er will they breathe such melody again!
Ne'er was a theme so genial to my heart
Ne'er was it so hard from any theme to part"
then left it all for the Windy City      to fall
down an elevator shaft "grievously crippled"
a *Century* rejection slip the final crushing blow

*Lyrics of Love* from a "poetaster's ill-tuned lyre"
while Bugbee changed the tone of historical writing
visited Colonel Bryan owned Estevan's archive
"stored in a tower room at his home in Quintana
to protect [it] from inundation by Gulf storms
more precious to him than a heritage of gold"
made headway on his Life then had to desist

238

Barker convinced that it would've been brilliant
but traveled to Junction for his failing health
his case diagnosed at Fort Bliss as tuberculosis
prescribed "rigorous exercise" as suitable care
"Despite their high appreciation of his services
the regents had no power to continue his salary
and the tragic pity was that he needed" the pay

"I am living a pretty hard life in El Paso
In Austin I at least deluded myself
into thinking that I passed for *somebody*
bank presidents would bow cordially
freshmen tip their hats    girls beam beamingly
but now as I pass along I hear
there goes another lunger    need a city ordinance

to keep them away    Have been packing grapes
with a family near Isleta    made with Dr. Baird
microscopic examinations    miss the classes
research on the Colony    can't imagine the University
on opening day    to be there when it starts
but to take no part"    at banks of the Rio Grande
on March 17, 1902 dead two months shy of 33

his hero of pneumonia in a December cold
at 43 on the 27th in his unheated shack
that last month there belatedly to draft
a proclamation against the slavery trade
by '36 its damage done then Bugbee gone
had just begun to save his rightful place
those with longer life with less to show

most with regrets for the wasted days
the owed unpaid    love unexpressed
points unrecalled of unsettled arguments
these without young to follow in their steps
how more often such offspring question
any stand not taken reject the one that is
all they long stood for & abided to bring

must wait for another to gird on the sword
who will seek in truth no revenge of time
will come only to recover the candid words
to copy documents & set straight the records
both those they wrote & the ways they lived
any justice self-fulfilled whose days deserve
a Barker born *en buena hora    el mío Cid*

Rio Grande

came never intending to leech off friends
but stayed for a week then half a year
cannot remember how or who invited
only where & why each yet stands clear
sleeping there on a daybed in between
a space heater & the back porch screen
with its plastic sheet flapped all night long
from the autumn & then the winter wind
one side freezing & the other done
merely existing at 2300 Rio Grande
a more real romantic self still in Chile
from where in September had just returned
there but a month though it seemed as if
had never left    worked on at Dacy's to earn
a trip would rejoin those divided selves
ready once more to quit this city
even seeing so plainly across 23rd
to where Elisa would first *tendu*
bending & stretching at that wooden bar
to lift & rise toward the balletic art
an inconceivable gift María would give
never thinking to look to Estevan's day
when he & afterwards General Lamar
had raised the schools & laid out roads
would pave the way for her training there
the slowly preparing for pains on pointe
knew only to toss & turn from hot to cold
on that mattress a thrall to such paradox
gripped by fears of how when or even if
by the icy lust smoldered deep within
for one with whom it wasn't meant
yet wondrously drawn to hurry back
through all that wrong to find the Beauty
the rightness of a ballerina born of her
whose *pas de chats* to piano strains
would bring her close as half a block
at ABT her classes first with Joanie
then once the studio moved to one on 5th
with Lisa Smith feather light as Juliet

& later still at Ballet Austin on Guadalupe
the renovated station of Hose Company No. 6
studying with Miss León & Mrs. Loomis
never guessed nor half surmised
the wars they fought with Santa Anna
Lipan Apache Karankaway the Comanche
the taxes levied & their soles replaced
would lead to a daughter's graceful steps
nor thought of Estevan's love repressed
his journey ending on a procrustean bed
his sacrifice unknown for all it was worth
for years this river-street crossed back & forth
sweating the German & the government tests
mostly concerned Verónica would hardly care
had abandoned place & people all for her
felt even as Lamar though hardly aware
when Mirabeau invaded Doña Carlota's land
marched to Monterrey from the Rio Grand'
to save that nation from its "erring mind"
by a sense of duty torn & pulled both ways
by the one he'd lost with his valiant sword
"But wo is me / Between us roars a gloomy stream"
while Villagrá captain-poet with Oñate's men
had paddled against its fateful current
trekking fiery sands untrod by Christian
through briars & savage nets of stinging twigs
lashing at eyes & ripping at armorless legs
their bare swollen feet at the mercy of
the scabrous rocks & high hot dunes
more than fifty days marched on & on
for seven straight in a drenching rain
at the end of a final four without a drop
in their haste the horses to overdrink
with their flanks filled dying "satisfied"
blinded by dagger sun & piñon lance
some waded out too far then swept away
by a wealth of waters could not believe
Oñate's men spread out along its banks
like bloated toads or tavern drunks
all this river to them not near enough
to slake their parched & voiceless throats

then at El Paso shown a convenient ford
by barbarians with the crudest instincts
hunting & fishing & living off roots
never breaking earth or planting seeds
unconcerned grand cities grew in far León
ignored the stir of palace or highest court
nor had they ever to face red tape
impediments to Oñate's moving ahead
delayed for months by jealous hatred
uncouth contented unsuspicious brutes
leading them across at the very point
where border guards would stop the car
on coming back from Juárez shopping
with a black sheep cousin & his Chicana wife
María still breast-feeding Darío then
the officer stooping to search inside
to ask Is everyone here a U.S. citizen
she a registered alien answered Chilean
when the trouble & rude treatment all began
her card left in Hobbs she could not come in
she & the baby must remain on that other side
"But wo is me / Between us roars a gloomy stream"
phoned to friends told them just break in
ransack the house to find that card
the one with her picture she detested so
whose magic numbers could divide Red Seas
would let them pass over & bring them back
the two kept there cut off so cruelly by
more than its waters by the indifferent law
while even those roomed along this street
would permit that passage to Beauty's home
its Spanish name a link to her long thin land
had strolled it with friends or all alone
to visit the shelves at Franklin Gilliam's
at 1913 on the corner somehow of 21st
his Brickrow Book Shop with Hardy & Howells
those first 1st editions had bought & read
a Spenser volume introduced by William Yeats
William Dean's novel *The Shadow of a Dream*
like the dark one fell on Estevan ever & again
along the way lost all but *Moments of Vision*

never a feeling those too were there & then
writing on the Hardy endsheet "Austin '61"
when would rib correct proper & superior Jon
with size thirteens among the yellowed leaves
rained down & stuck to his heels on misted walks
shrill grackles whistling in the bare-limbed trees
their wet black branches darkening against
the gray-orange-pink of autumn's sunset sky
gave hope even here a poem could come to life
long before nights on that screened-in porch
when Mary Jane tired of seeing a poet-type
asleep out there or in her kitchen scribbling
or ironing a dress shirt for work each morning
she cooking Hickey's breakfast & chatting a bit
to be civil even thinking Why doesn't he leave
but stayed on in '65 through fall & winter
a nuisance to them though would always pay
yet how could 25 dollars ever cover the sight
of being there whenever they returned each night
to pass through that "bedroom" & enter their own
at least had used the toilet & shower at Lonn's
his garage apartment back of their big two-storey
nextdoor to Leslie who would loan her phone
a bother to all but still each putting up with
the savings made & the moonings for love
in the meantime butt of their Elephant jokes
once gone appropriated the Spiller & Baugh
those expensive hardback literary histories
could feel no rancor to lose such books
for not even those would ever repay
the inconvenience of such a wornout stay
only wish this perhaps may compensate
if those times with all their impositions
their kindnesses & "moments of vision"
will bring at least a painful pleasure
beyond any imbursement of a costlier kind
by allowing these sketches of former days
to make small return for all they gave
for theirs as worthy if written up right
as the lives & letters in that reference set
Hickey in cowboy boots & bluejean pants

all he would wear unless his Stetson
as in between polishing each paragraph
he would lift his bare mole-ridden back
in a heave to catch his second breath
like his hero Fitzgerald he couldn't spell
signed up for a course to get some help
his name noticed on that remedial roll
by the Dean took away his assistantship
afterwards at the Student Union holding forth
on the latest fictive or linguistic theory
holing up at the house on Rio Grande
seated day & night in that booklined study
taking a deep drag a swig from his Pepsi
shutting himself off by those sliding doors
to correct & retype his Texas stories
of buttering tortillas or hunting quail
the authentic life & death of Smiley Logan
who at 12 hit Odessa's National Bank
at 25 by a truckload of underfed steers
his best of a TV newsman in San Antone
a Jewish "ambulance chaser" met his match
in the Mexican mother of George Guzmán
viewed the slow dying filmed & shown
unflinching in the face of that car wreck's jaws
of her own son there seen pinned within
for her the newsman's re-run a canticle
Marlinberg the priest who offered it up
such scenes Hickey meant for the magazines
*The New Yorker  Harper's   The Atlantic*
looking ever East for the acceptance signs
gave it all up when they hadn't arrived
later his tale of a nude rancher dies in a tub
listed by McMurtry in *In a Narrow Grave*
but merits a place on this roll call more
for bringing them out as Estevan before
lines & pages of native or immigrant alike
edited for *Riata* & given welcome at home
where authors & artists all gathered to meet
came in a steady stream to this river-street
prose & pigment talk overflowing the rooms
their canvases hung where Mary Jane served

as gracious host to the unwashed anarchists
a Gilbert Shelton showing off a latest t-shirt
featuring Wonder Wart Hog's bristling snout
known too for drawing that satirical Ranger
a stunted Hairy with long holstered six-guns
such figures created for his serial cartoons
their comments made in social & political fun
or with Hairy pictured on that *Ranger* cover
peering up at a Mona Lisa bore his ugly mug
in its caption spouting to the museum guard
he didn't know nothin' 'bout no *modren* art
but by god he knew he liked what he saw
& Jaxson's underground *Rag* the nation's first
was it he who drew that so classic strip
of Lester's finger-lickin' good fried chicken
of that owner wielding his racist lumber
whose attitude toward his Negro cook
got radically adjusted by Super Good
but not before the hero's battered & bruised
by Maddox's axe-handle answer to protest
when a light bulb goes on over Super's head
he'll take a black indelible ink & dye the bigot
& so many others like Manske Osborn & Beeson
Harold's "A Matter of Possession" written
in a room rented together summer of '63
just around the block from the Robert E. Lee
down from a bar Morton would regularly frequent
after practice walking along 21st past the Littlefield
Coppini's web-footed horses above its sudsy fountain
reminded Mort of a *Lone Star* longneck & a sour pickle
home by the watered lawns of those frail landladies
tough customers those when it came time to collect
ran their musty boarding houses on the up & up
served creamed cauliflower & plenty of spuds
though couldn't hold out against the push for space
another house & street forever displaced
another memoried address has given way
yet won't let go though there's not a trace
as when Sugar & Turpin were both released
right when Clarence's turn had come at last
to claim as throne that jail cell's single chair

but with neither to see him its meaning lost
when he would rip the legs & kick the seat
laughing burn them all in hysterical defeat
& though to most it won't matter one bit
leveled will hold to their image the more
a character in Carolyn's "Ancient History"
her early story from *Riata* spring of '64
crazy old Miss Agnes Doyle to a prissy girl
hell no she don't have no telephone
& all you need's a good switchin'
declares "Of the two kinds of not knowing
not knowing where you've been is worse"
Hickey printing others by Branda & Giles
not then Jim's tale of Whitman's "August Day"
came later with its "landscape of Spanish-brick
fountains and statuary ranging from lifeless"
to "the bloody mangled bodies in his wake"
but rather poems by Wally Stopher the 3rd
by Tom Whitbread came to sit one night
on the edge of that daybed there out back
with a party at the Hickeys' roaring inside
had not then given it up    spoke under the effects
of what it might have been too sleepy to catch
most likely of the trains he so truly loves
from the third number of *Triad* can hear his lines
take to task a *Harper's* "reporter/distorter"
of these streets & the Texas Eagle's diner car
Wally last seen bound east on a campus shuttle
snaggletoothed & needing the price of a string
said without a guitar it kept him from singing
wondered without his teeth had his talent gone
or with less to begin with had been better off
just picking it up rather from all these others
or "for a song" as laureate Barney has said
in these "certain discoverable neighborhoods"
here on Estevan's river & numbered streets
from Hickey's contributors like Mueller Lewis
whose haunting "Homespun Idyll" forever weaves
how Buddo turns from spider to a victim trapped
in his own triumph in his own sabotage web
or from Eldon rediscovered Christina Stead

then caught up ten years in revising the facts
for *The Handbook of Texas* set his novel aside
to verify names of odd townships now owe to him
Fono bringing over "Circus" by Frigyes Karinthy
after he escaped from his Hungary invaded by tanks
on Rio Grande without exception received & accepted
& later on 12th at Hickey's gallery called naturally
after Papa's story "A Clean Well-Lighted Place"
like a selfless Estevan Dave promoting their work
till he up & left it for old New York
predictably losing to that tempting Big Apple
his lovely Eve from Midland-Odessa
with her deep accent forever distinctive
its desert sweetness so clear & clean
not oil slick as her Permian Basin
but welling up as if artesian
rich in its unassuming ingenuous ring
looked back from another hot business trip
an exhibit in Omaha Chicago or Nashville
to lose her among the lonely office halls
watched as his Eurydice half disappeared
into a known attorney's awaiting arms
saw his own employment evaporate too
he an agent then for the pop art rage
that famous quote his parting shot
at the boss had gone & double-crossed
him & all of his painter friends
"the ship abandoned a sinking rat"
while Estevan never left except for them
to carry their case to a congressional session
gave up those plans for erecting his home
putting up Mary Holley & hearing her voice
digging their garden to her strummed guitar
"I entered upon the busy stage of life
with ideas which had they been true
would have made this Earth a paradise
dreams of youth unpoisoned by ambition
my angel Mother kind hearted father
my first standards of human nature
wealth was not the incentive led me here
*Ambition* kindled its fires in my breast

but the flame was a mild and gentle one
consisting more of the wish to build up
the others' fortunes and happiness
asylum for sufferers from selfish avarice
the mania for speculation
and you my friend
how shall I ever thank you
for venturing into this wilderness
how express the happiness
of the ten days visit
Gardens and rosy bowers
and ever verdant groves
music books and intellectual amusements
can all be ours
Millions could not buy them
but the right disposition with competence
insure them"
his words intended for María too
spoken as well of whoever endured
a shameless poet the way Lonn did
as days turned into weeks & months
of shaving & bathing & listening to
his recording of a Prokofieff ballet
*Cinderella* foretelling Elisa's *plié*
chiming a warning it was time to go
his classical collection surprising so
even more his mind on hearing that drawl
his by far the deepest guttural
a snorting infectious high-pitched laugh
no idle claim of "nowhere but Texas"
consumed by the case bock Shiner beer
knew state politics from Schulenberg to Freer
could speak to the meaning of a post-oak fence
Virginia worm    zig-zag    split-rail    stake & rider
each "impervious to cattle hogs or high winds"
"a more handsome ornament than the chain-link"
suddenly his booming voice turning sentimental
as it pleaded with Leslie to go for a pitcher
down at Scholz Garten before they'd close
when her text of *Child Psych* fell to the floor
& would squeeze as a threesome in his VW Bug

was she first mentioned the book by Griffith
her ex-teacher on a Dickinson under duress
its "Long Shadow" cast for all these years
her own too who saw to it others got through
lent moral support before that call to Chile
& afterwards when it came to a choice
set her lovelife aside to listen & serve
as a Sacajawea for guiding safely across
yet what solace can these memories be
a re-run of collisions have mostly outlived
of survivors changed from young & cocky
so certain their plans would all work out
in some ways turned out for the better
if for the worse can retracing a stream
reverse where waters ran out of control
in a blind moment dragged so quickly down
with the rudder gone why recover a paddle
in remembrance can a river yet hope to renew
in holding to it won't it only grow stagnant
no answers to show only this lifted footage
this spring tide of a gratitude flows on & on

# San Gabriel

with the north fork out of its banks
as it pushed & gushed to gain the Gulf
felt another flood of past impressions
gathering force from this final street
swept up in all has branched out from it

crossed the highway's concrete bridge
saw in the rushing & raging below
broken limbs & the tops of trees
ragweed tips & the johnson grass
grown tall along this river's edge

swayed in the relentless swollen wind
of waters beyond the depth of any
María there at home awaiting word
had made it safely    had gotten through
so fearful after days of unceasing rain

with engines stalled & drivers trapped
then washed away    only caught up in
thrown off by all there was to sing
carried by visions beyond her reach
of years spent here before she came

men & women suddenly gone forever
in Shoal Creek's unimagined torrent
beneath the Colorado's deceptive calm
so happy to have her worrying there
never for the hurt it would give to her

but to know such care still coursing
in veins as in those vows exchanged
when was driven to her faroff shores
to become with her a more than one
that meeting set by routes & trails

passage taken over sands & seas
the endless caravans & caravels
of such pioneers & conquistadors
arriving apart then brought together
though on that day had gone alone

passing a systems plant of IBM
the entrance to Texas Instruments
condominiums & shopping centers
suburbs once their hunting grounds
paved parking lots their cedar hills

surrounding family & plentiful fruit
a garrison facing to the hostile side
defense against the dread Apache
missions built to bring them in
irrigation from its delicious stream

tribes in their "natural inconstancy"
drawn off dependably years at a time
by an occult power no padre divined
awaited each day the children's return
Hierbipiame Mayeye Deadose Yojuane

came again though never for long
their destroyers no enemy Lipans
rather the fathers' measles & pox
meaning to save yet in the end
sent them down to sooner defeat

river where buffalo & Tonkawa roamed
named first for Xavier one more saint
by those had it most in mind to change
the religious course of their native life
while turning the arid fields to fertile

Ranchería Grande to receive the Word
along with fanegas beans & chilis
from Spain's official King & Queen
every 12 or 15 days a butchered bull
only felt blessed with bellies full

"luxuries are inventions or phantasms
we can invent and give reins to fancy
in Texas as well as any where else"
his vision reaching past Brushy Creek
though no sign now of their coming back

on through Lampasas    San Saba    Brady
to a desolate town called somehow Eden
stopped the Volks at its chain cafe
where the single waitress taking orders
on being asked to change a dollar

gave back the least celestial look
then phoned ahead to San Angelo
another town christened by Catholic faith
served the deep needs of those among
the earliest to come from Mexico

called Gerald Lacy from that paradise
said would be delayed in getting in
jested that spot was hard to leave
though never deny the magnetism
the long pull of a people & place

at the native's mind & body
as of this river enraged in spring
can erode with unreasoning allure
torn at forever by town after town
groves & orchards of pecan & peach

by plowed fields on treeless plains
stretching flat under caprock skies
taking them in as a dream come true
a love affair no criminal past
no present wrongs can quite undo

from Fort Concho in the 1880s
a buffalo soldier at McDonald's saloon
a Black private there to dance for drinks
a San Saban told him Don't you stop
the unarmed trooper did    the sheepman shot

"indicted for murder in the first degree
and transferred for trial to Austin
the jurors had scarcely left their seats
before they'd brought the verdict in: not guilty
and the 'matter passed into history'"

no am not out to make this another job
like the one advised by an army surgeon
"the privies attached to the barracks
should be white-washed and disinfected
the slop barrels with Carbolic acid"

look back now to the form it's taken
a Satan surveys his troops in their fall
recall the street of this river's name
its heaven inhabited at times by hell
a pained awareness of the little given

on review in that uniform can feel it itch
can hear Mary's letter dated 8th of June
heartily sick of the old world's doings
tyrannies great & small     their cruelties
fill her with abhorrence of self & species

prays he be firmly opposed to servitude
longs so for the peace of a simple life
"will admit no debasing passions"
no longer to seek for over much
for cannot then be disappointed

he writing of retiring & settling down
but fears even then in spite of himself
will be "borne along on the course of events
into a stormy and troubled sea
the past is but a picture

a shadow of various hues     the future
we know not what     theological and myth-
ological contradictions     inconsistencies
make it everything anything nothing"
remembers her injunction

"'laugh away care' . . . Adios amiga mia"
& again ten days hence
in "a melancholy void"
she he says "must fill it"
sees them together out on ponies

scampering down to the beach
over & across the flowering prairies
between the water's wide expanse
a green carpet the woods enfringe
friendship   happiness   but then

lets "that chord alone"
switches to economy & plainness
"Heaven help us from extremes"
"keep in view the dark as well as the bright
if disappointment come it then will be

deprived of a part of its sting"
& after Valentines the taciturn man
grown loquacious in writing again
is fond & frank & signs himself
with "a long farewell"

but where does a river begin
for a start have pinned it down
to San Gabriel Street & that rented room
yet how many others for reaching there
& beyond to all the unmeasured then

in '33 Mary said of a Brazos branch
"salt enough to pickle pork
never overflows its banks" then in '34
its mouth obstructed by a narrow bar
the kind can always form from sand

lost it all   cattle & corn
& before that flood the cholera
rampage set them back some seven years
here by the bills & the children ill
excuses when little or nothing came

borne off course by divergent views
cowed by events might misrepresent
& how discount the thinnest tributary
north at Amon Carter's old Fort Worth
May Street's last full block at Berry

told its tales in sketches left unfinished
of each house with its own to tell
Keetch's three for wife & daughters
the middle one bought by Alvin & Sis
the grandest moved from way uptown

near Throckmorton ran by Standard Printing
mother & dad's shop in '40 before the war
before big outfits forced them out of business
put to sleep there with teddy on a paper bin
at that rented house fed cards in a toy press

from its backyard flew missions round the globe
dials & controls on an apple crate crayon drawn
grounded for having taken off before the nap
for setting a match to grass on railway tracks
smoke signals read by firemen doused the blaze

returned to those rooms with tonsils removed
mother almost sick from the vomited ether
dad's bought-&-paid-for shetland undelivered
tuned in there to Sky King & ordered his ring
glowed in the dark hid within its secret code

waded on that corner lot Nan's double pond
where goldfish lurked under its lily pads
her patio with its redwood monkey works
Kung Fu statue between two sticky cypress
his speech of waters off a cast iron tongue

by dawn already pulling her moss & weeds
stoked limbs in her black woodburning stove
baked canned biscuits dipped in butter
melted brown sugar floated fresh pecans
in morning air the incense of her cooking

while across the way at Terry Timmons' home
Kimbrough set her dial for the Breakfast Club
to march with Don McNeil round the dining table
his granny with her napkined *Coke* or *Dr. Pepper*
needed with George & Annie Ruth gone to Jesus

when Uncle Jimmy couldn't hold a job
her son with his vivid lies of Pacific isles
an Audie Murphy behind the enemy lines
captured a machine gun nest singlehanded
Argonne forest heroics boys clamored for

not the neighbor girls knew sex & horses
climbed up after in Nan's sprawling vitex
fought with one day    made up the next
games begun by choosing up sides
to chase & catch till nightfall

the hide & seek of their tanned aroma
puzzled by how they could differ so
at Halloween gave the spookiest parties
led blindfolded by their softer hands
to feel wet grapes    said They're eyeballs

even Beauty seen by the light of their lamp
recognized later by those sights & sounds
before she had stitched her tapestried past
before Ovalle first heard her mandolin voice
her photo developing in that alchemical wash

armies chosen on Hemphill at the five-&-ten
masks & costumes turned pirate or goblin
nickle-&-dime dreams unawakened from
White Theatre stars still show the way
boarded buses to ad posters stay & stay

their Don't Get Off still rings in ears
each day there yet a drop or a trickle
a deeper immersion in the poem to be
those rills collected to a roaring river
poured southward here to Estevan's city

257

rivulets forking or joining once more
then touching within at San Gabriel
the miracle of how in each man may flow
the rivers of when & wherever he's been
points north or south never meant to meet

met in the meaning of the memory stream
as out of the sand & the prickly pear
came again that summer from Hebbronville
carrying within Cowtown's Trinity River
its zoo miniature train & ferris wheel

down two doors from 19th to house them all
to live at one with those ships at port
tankers dribbling rust in the Neches bend
driven by on workdays at Spector's store
Guarantee Shoes by the tracks on Pearl

feet fit from every walk of Beaumont life
keeping company along this final street
took its name from that bridge's river
brings back that summer returned to rent
from Dave Hickey's friend Bill Faulkner

Dave's coeditor acting a manager's part
Hickey editing & contributing to *Riata* then
with Whitbread the three doing *Triad* too
had come earlier with a piece on Gertrude
accepted for a '63 Lost Generation issue

as from that time & that rented room
through a backward glance's biblical rock
see how the writing would spill & spray
from there sent drifting down by Dave
through literally miles of marked essays

1906    the same address introduced
Debabrata Ghosh lived 3 blocks north
geneticist vegetarian & a fan of Tagore
would hit him up for the Chilean trip
its denouement of that awkward kiss

& what would Estevan's reaction have been
approved such a loan toward puppy love
opponent of "the mania for speculation"
the taking a chance with Ghosh's hundred
another from Popo & three from Alums

had to outright lie for the largest chunk
when an agency reported no credit rating
no bank about to fund any venture south
with Dacy's conspicuous deposit pouch
talked big business    a tall investment tale

an Indian researcher a Roma teacher-rancher
ex-students enamored of rampant Longhorns
a loan officer deaf to such mushy romance
these footed the fare through Panama City
a landing in Lima & a last stop at Cerrillos

Santiago's airport reunion had shelled out for
disappointing after months of dreaming it there
in the end the scheme a failure the Garden cursed
& what would they have said    Told you so
their money gone for that bubble burst

their savings spent for a pair unsuited
traveling by train in her Citroneta
to Puntiagudo Quillota or Viña del Mar
high interest paid for the finding there
a difference as between Pacific & Andes

her family *fundo* with its brand of cheese
a silver bell tinkled for the Mapuche maids
taught them the use of their sewing machine
lived out back somewhere behind the kitchen
with hands red from serving hers softly gloved

"agriculture cattle raising and other labors
to which they're dedicated could not be carried on
without the aid of the robust and indefatigable
arms of that race of the human species
who to their misfortune suffer slavery"

259

then proved a serendipitous trip
as the anguish & bitter regret
all earned the returns so unexpected
directed as though by a destiny led
to María's modest home on Pyramid

to her house there gave its welcome
when weak with vermin was taken in
her sister cooking the curative meals
her nanny washing the plates & sheets
& Beauty giving up her place to sleep

brought boiled apples & spaghetti with oil
their loans reaping then such dividends
the banker's & those of Exes & friends
guided to fruition from San Gabriel
by a knock so startling at 2 a.m.

on opening that door & standing in shorts
to hear the news Bill McReynolds brought
elected to follow in Dave's legendary steps
the mantle passed or the proverbial buck
trembled with joy shook with thinking ahead

before that had wandered in a morbid frame
ups & downs of numbered & river-streets
stepping unsurely by those fragrant blooms
in search of a flowering might correspond
lend relief from a withering shriveling mind

found for a while at that rooming house
at 905 West 22nd among Louis's friends
his closest the Indian failed prelims twice
others taught Hindustani at meatless meals
to fix them a ritual ever beginning with rice

observed until at Lupe's Spanish Village
found even refried beans strictly forbidden
since cooked in a prohibited animal fat
when craved again that indigenous diet
the strength it gave not alone ingredients

in Lou's one room in that gabled home
see him re-read Dickens' *Edwin Drood*
would crib from him to fear no prose
yet never to praise the story he wrote
of a Scotsman wedded to an octoroon

or another printed in *Corral* for '63
of a lonely figure his spitting image
an office worker in a dry goods store
too shy to approach the cute salesgirl
unseen from his balcony sends down to her

her customers' change in a metal cyclinder
spying on her from above is self-despised
in his mirror at night finding a deep façade
while Lou to spend each dreary weekend
doing his reserve duty at camp in Killeen

he a better writer than admitted then
out of jealousy or have his words & themes
with time improved    matured    come to
after all these years & the realization
it takes much more than supposed it would

as Estevan's story has gained with age
hired out to work in those mines of lead
so determined to pay off his every debt
the one for Butler's Arkansas slaves
"harassed him more than any event"

not knowing how deeply they went
liabilities to Louis & his Hindi friends
the worst of all usurped from him
he in his loneliness so in need of them
how ever in the world to make it up

compounded more with each return
in front of a Burns blind from birth
necked with Andrea who wore his ring
as Esteven declared "a cruel affair
have never known so base a man"

fissures opening where seemingly safest
limestone rests on pre-cretaceous
belongs properly to the Potomac series
approaches San Gabriel at 28th
jointed fractured weathered but there

& then at 24th will abruptly stop
but don't be fooled for it reappears
at 22nd just above in a blue clay bluff
a Fort Worth limestone on down the hill
Pease Park where their cork would pop

Jim's champagne toast to getting engaged
later his marriage flat as an opened bottle
as shark teeth at 12th begin showing up
another clay Eagle Ford the last outcrop
of *Exogyra arietina*'s greenish tint

scratched beneath their surface stripes
to identify an instinct for survival apart
predatory as any in love    exposes a
greater diversity of chalky deposits
than in any other area of equal extent

in that science received a D at Lamar
repeating it here only to start & drop
blamed indifference of a lab instructor
marked off for misspelling a pteropod
he himself had to use the textbook for

slid down Shoal Creek "slippery as soap"
in dress pants so expensive to dry-clean
slopping through pasture mud at Pilot Knob
to a submarine volcano as each class before
so resenting a search for the long explored

& though in these friends there's nothing new
alone or in composite find them all unique
feldspathic & pyroxene blends soon to end
with each of them    extinct as any species
inspiring attempts at a lasting pentastich

262

wanted from the first to trace their ways
dynamical geologics of the present time
repudiating fossil fates had to memorize
out to retain the vitality of a living line
uncover the record of their Texas lives

later re-reading that course's lessons
to find such crystalline faces intact
under pressure their past compacted
striking even embedded pyrite phrases
in layers assayed prove highest grade

metamorphic in their giving a shape
to any nugget a stanza contains
feelings solidified from that earlier day
in mingling magma with reason's cold
to cool the passion for deceptive gold

most at 1906 Apt. C of this closing street
though it form nowhere on Waller's map
part of that first mayor's city plat
& yet so prominently has figured in
while hastening here there to & from

longer this side of campus than any other
except for that set of garage apartments
on Poplar by Alpha Epsilon Pi
where "hey Bernie throw me the ball"
is a yell still hangs on high

at each & every address to know again
named & unnamed will forever owe
Morton with his heart-warming humor
Jim whose visual puns on prickly pear
have drawn the eyes to others' poems

Jon who sketched that sitting there
knew Andy on Poplar as never before
fell out with George & the Science Org
heard red-headed David at his violin
as if foretelling Vivaldi & Darío's bow

263

Morton rooming then across 19th
sharing his taste for bottled brew
for jazz solos from that Golden Age
drinking to Bix's piano on "In a Mist"
NORK Red Nichols the amazing Miff

"the foursquare same-way-every-time
ragtime feel" of the ODJB style
Dutrey   Kid Ory   & Vernon's own
trombonists in that dated tradition
licks Stine imitated to keep it alive

a product of Big T's stomping grounds
& born like Teagarden to travel around
a Wichita Falls transplant to eastern roots
though back then after a quart to introduce
a pride in his place's western twang

at Shakey's Pizza Parlor dixied nights
at 31st & Guadalupe his old-time tone
his straight-ahead drive revives this need
to play it "For No Reason at All in C"
to rhythm & rhyme Estevan's city

when the frats laughed for cuddliest dates
howled & guffawed at Chaplin's tramp
Morton would find them too offensive
an affront to the comedy he deeply loved
"nothing" he said "can be that funny"

knew too well the sadness beneath
his own covered up by Mercutian wit
would clasp both hands against his chest
breathe deeply & release the heaviest sigh
Norma Shearer kissing his poisoned lips

visiting later in Hobbs on Yeso Street
his french horn forgotten behind the car
backed out & crumpled its costly bell
took it with the stoic poise of a comic
his remake of a flick by Laurel & Hardy

listening then in that ell-shaped room
where one weekend "Spillway" came
the *Riata* logo in a morning dream
envisioned it from bottles labeled
with Anheuser-Busch's eagled A

but an R instead with curling rattler
before that awoke to conceive a cover
a crude landscape with a yucca plant
underneath an oriental sort of sunset
but required an artist could render that

crossed the campus to find Ralph White
he a professor in the Department of Art
its far-off building unentered till then
its turpentine & paint-fumed halls
easels sporting nudes in charcoal & oils

sent for a student nearly no one knew
drove with Jim in his vintage DeSoto
at the Tavern on 12th to have a few
discuss the design had come to mind
to discover in him the one & only

warm bright & eager & from Amarillo
poor & working his way through school
rented just up the hill off Blanco
across from the old Military Institute
a blacksmith shop turned a cheap one-room

those the training grounds for making do
where the endless arguments all began
over deadlines & each one's differing view
at the drawing board night after night
bent with his twitching eye ever intent

where bare rock walls & roof beams
reeked of smoke & the dampened ash
though his fireplace rarely if ever lit
barely affording food much less wood
yet his own brain a glowing smithy

265

burned three days & nights in a row
forged again & again each layout page
pulling it all up & starting over
stuck iron back in & pumped the bellows
hammered & plunged & tempered

was driven crazy    just wanted it done
had not "checked haste urges men to mar
the dignity of every act"    rush into print
then regret the flaws    can never learn
from Dante from Estevan from a patient Jim

"men of enlightened judgement
unshaken perseverance integrity of purpose
calmly put their shoulders to the wheel
toil for the good of others without their trying
to force it forward prematurely"

those who take their time
who make it serve for more
longer hours than others require
to see the contract worded right
position better the artwork & type

their loss of sleep another's reward
the accuracy of their selfless touch
with a craft & care can alchemize
till weeks & months have all paid off
achieve a placement wins the award

though not without demands they make
kept awake through half those nights
holding a flashlight aimed & steady
from buckboard wheel to sketch pad
crawling for details out in the dark

as if a Euryalus & Nisus off on sortie
through Rutulian ranks deadly to both
their enemies undone by Bacchus & dice
then weighted down by too much booty
delayed by cutting of their bloody swath

when caught by Volcens & returning guards
one's neck a bright flower the mower lops
the other speared to bleed wine-red drops
on his beloved friend's so luckless corse
incomparable scene yet no dearer than this

in a fraternity's yard with stinging nettles
with its Roundup party still a bash inside
its antique buggy parked out on the grass
stretched on stomachs to catch its spokes
real but superimposed on a '90s mustache

Jim's synthesis done as illustration for
Bratcher on Crane's stories set in Texas
he writing on while his Cherokee wife
kept very well at the house expecting
took her fresh bouquets to be let in

to the aroma of her homebaked bread
would buy him a quart of any brand
to keep him going    stayed on & on
through every wry & sober sentence
paragraphed better with abundant drink

afterwards went for drawing the gun
to Memorial Museum on San Jacinto
a revolver by Colt or some Remington
another piece in Jim's puzzle picture
barrel & liveoak framing a cumulate face

all Stephen's typical western motifs
captured by the artist's pencil & pen
that frat house's weathered carriage
transferred as they slapped & bragged
Bratcher acting the part of pumpkin eater

all locked in a tray inked & printed
to be let out by whoever's read    "far
straight shadows in back of the stars"
an essay view to those Grecian echoes
not another pledge class but Sophoclean

267

though even so the prop was theirs
supplied a likeness above the cravat
adding their bit to Stephen's collar
beyond their booze has long worn off
if unconscious contributed all the same

can claim at most the handpunched holes
for his Asian sunburst    licking & sticking
of red seals on black overlapping ribbons
paid for again out of all but empty pockets
for another striking cover of Jim's design

thanks to Bratcher earning a little extra
by tutoring of swimming & diving teams
he so upset by "No Perching Allowed"
had no patience with such inane antics
just because Zuk wasn't invited to read

short-tempered stocky & so outspoken
could never understand that one position
though still return to the words he wrote
his helping of athletes at every hour
his Cherokee happy inside her shell

all integrated then through meticulous Jim
a single instance yet repeated time & again
in '81 to punch his bookmarks for *Washing*
three colored ribbons would trim & lay in
photos pasted for *Strangers* by Sandra Lynn

o cannot complain would do it over & over
though never can it be as it was back then
with fights waged nightly on *Mountain Dew*
when it first turned out as Jim had planned
a work affirmed by the Chancellor's summons

how many swigs taken for making it through
*Texan* letters damned it as a Christmas tree
the whole idea of any East-West issue
a waste of every student's blanket fee
how often thought to throw in the towel

& then with it out to receive the call
from Ransom's Tower now brings to mind
Yeats pacing his battlements of history & myth

peering from his ancient Gaelic pile
to where a blind man's song revealed
all hearts since Helen have been betrayed

to this of Cret's design blind Borges came
feeling the walls where Whitman's deadly aim
dropped Eckman's son    others far as Guadalupe

Telémakhos' room with its circular view
his private place to ponder alone
that hope held out by Athena's words

though Dobie set no store
by this Greek erection
this impotent prick of imported style

saw it merely as one more sign
have always had to find inferior
whatever is here on ranch or range

any dogtrot architecture
& yet before its clock tolls one
stirred each Friday by its carillons

ring Brahms' variations across the Mall
or at night on leaving stadium gates
gaze up with shameful joy

at its columnar top
to its glowing orange
for victorious sports

here had searched in vain
through winning football seasons from '60 on
for the smallest gains over a vast unknown

seeking in its morgue-like catalog
a living food for a brain half-starved
fingering the stained file cards

forever hopeful    forever lost
so baffled by Dewey    by the new LC
then entered at last the holy of holies

these stacks still closed to the undergrad
couldn't ride a shaky elevator to dim-lit floors
emblems in themselves of a groping start

worse before that first degree
permitted the ascent upon one's own
among broken backs to explore alone

until then having to fill a slip
a request handed over at the checkout desk
to haughty clerks looked to know it all

those deep needs sought by unseen hands
dropped from above by a pulleyed box
clanked & screeched as it brought them down

volumes lowered to the sophomore
more sacred showing up at that sliding door
as though untouched

tomes ever taking longer to read
than death-like due dates stamped in red
& with no assurance would understand

even getting through no guarantee
would discover the key could open
decipher the meaning of any chapter

confounded further
made to suffer evermore
for wanting just to know

or wrote the wrong call numbers
saw 8 for 3
I for T

those letters drawn
by student drones
became in '61 another cog

hired by the hour to prepare the cloth
to print them straight & clear
that a shelver not misplace the title

such confusion might have aided
in passing through to the unsuspected
if learned at all ever learned too late

the new publications considered best
their bindings so clean & smooth
on them the ink adhered with ease

not so with those were old & brittle
their authors too
if never assigned never looked into

pens gouging their softened spines
words beading up on greasy leather
or slick from use in a backward time

untrained in calligraphy or fixative sprays
the figures coming out too large or small
blinded the eyes in the o's & e's

at their loaded trucks others seated
foreigners mostly     art majors
a precise machine-like Japanese

an Eastern European
Nowotny by name
a Dean of Students had the same

she a divorcee with a child at home
who read those early stumbling tries
telling of how she picked up Spanish

selling on the side her debit policies
attended classes first then labeled on
such a bore she said but had her son to feed

little thought where that search would lead
to what way-stations
what cornices on the journey "up"

full circle to the HRC
even with critics all faithfully read
to return unlettered

back to where it all began
the rare collections    first housed them here
at the Tower's base in whispering rooms

Harry Huntt Ransom's bargain buys
books correspondence & manuscripts
iconography galleys & page proofs

scholars & workers so cramped for space
Bracker cataloging the Christopher Morley
in a converted kitchen beside the sink

mixed him up with a writer of Shakespeare's age
another error    another unknown figure
then revealed by friendship with his avid fan

showed verses in tribute to Dorothy Wordsworth
a preface to Whitman    Hazlitt's sense of place
men so admired by the Argentinean

in style Borges & Morley Americas apart
yet one in their love of those earlier minds
had come here first to find another

Sir Walter & his History of the World
written when his Queen had him condemned
to gaze from the tower on Virginia grass

the Ocean Shepherd's fickle Faery
Ralegh's own hard-hearted Scinthia
her loyal knight even there to pen

a poem so difficult still to enter
the one Spenser's Colin mentions
come home again to Kilcolman

his allegory of that hidden stream
had filled the library's orangy forms
in hopes somehow those might let in

unlock that courtier's imprisoned thought
its rolling record of earth & time
in his expansive Elizabethan prose

his tongue though kept
enclosed in stone
could yet by way

of that state where Estevan
first drew breath
perhaps imagine this cedared air

before that call had roomed with George
friends since junior high
together in classes or dance band practice
in Demolays or on tournament trips
to the speech & orchestra contests

camping overnight with Lloyd Lejeune
a trio among the muscadine
in a grove by Texas Gulf Sulphur's mine
just down that shell-paved road
from George's step-dad's burger stand

served the best ground cuts of chuck or round
cattycorner to the South Park Drive-In
a block from the monument to Spindletop
a photo of it framed in his Houston home
with its broken blade of a towering spout

suspended then more than three score years
against that vacant coastal sky
a black ray of rising rain
unlike its profits has yet to fall
unfailing as the goulash his mother served

tented together in woods where Cubby ran
barking in circles all night long
at noises out in the frightening dark
crackling sticks & rustling leaves
with dawn surrounded by cattle stared in

on the Fourth sold fireworks down the way
from the gusher had burst & showered all
fenced-in with a marker to keep the date
of the Boom meant mammon's almighty dollar
shot off cherry bombs thought to rival

deaf to all the jobs it brought
knew it more as a favorite spot
littered by *Trojans* the parkers tossed
engaged then rather in religious love
snubbed those after the bucks & bods

lacked any notion of all its worth
how pumps had piped the paychecks
for Estevan's beloved language school
for tenured professors damned to death
all but idolized in the very same breath

how rigs had plunged the diamond bits
had fueled the tribute Barker built
to honor Estevan's "thorough greatness"
papers Bugbee brought through R.L. Batts
studied with the Southern Fund of Littlefield

those interest-gathering long-term notes
that Major left for collecting a wrongful past
who outdrew a hired gun in the Civil War
spared a druggist had hoarded liquor
admitted Ferguson's firing Battle a big mistake

paying silver outside the polling booths
for every proper Negro vote
sheer folly to him the shipping of beef
north & east when later the state
would buy it back in imported steaks

this other George never thought in fortunes
would raise stud horses in Arkansas
teaching there until divorce & then reupped
when in Korea stationed near the DMZ
later in Palestine cooked his mother's recipes

tried something new most every week
growing as always tired of each
the latest gear gimmick fad or trick
a computer watch played Sinclair's "Eyes"
an acetyline cannon scared Andy shitless

with Jimmy Hayes in that '52 Henry J
the three drove round in Beaumont days
when underneath innocent Andy's seat
had hidden that flame-throwing mechanism
screamed as it roared & blazed at his feet

George showing off gadgets found or bought
anything to amaze a friend or adversary
a Depression souvenir from an Ozark farm
an uncle picked it up where George was born
Goose Creek under its coat of varnish

mostly known for those practical jokes
though never laughed at his hometown's name
would pass the toughest exams in early teens
first in the class with a driver's license
the first to earn his ham operator's

funny his taking to heart that photograph
of a phone company captured long before
its building-shack he had never seen
yet a call to something so deep within
only coming through on Poplar Street

that part of him an untapped well
blew in by nitroglycerin of a bitter dispute
a debate unlike those forensic speeches
he'd prepared for his & Jimmy's team
when were given topics so meaningless

whether to pay farmers not to plant
should a nuclear freeze begin or cease
what's the safest way to make world peace
in education which should it be
more science math or humanities

little to do with a preference test
when the candidates first squared off
to him Nixon ever had the upper hand
knew what to say his style superior
could keep Kennedy for all he cared

was like that choice in a certain way
a fireworks display over real or fake
set off those loud painsgiving cracks
loaded words exploding in sensitive ears
in one another's darkened hardened face

had blown up in defense of him
attacked his friends attended the Org
swore their testimonies insincere
George standing up for all of them
then moved out & took a single room

off Nueces down from The Barkley Arms
with its polished brass & hotel awning
an art major dubbing that rooming house
"The Armpit"    painted for it that sign
faced it east to Dirty's hamburger joint

widowed Mrs. Ninks its blind landlady
with her roof & second floor rotting away
one boarder entered & stepped right through
she listening close for the stairs to creak
for students would sneak out not to pay

later on would learn of his Science group
how he'd never meant so much to them
nothing close to a bivouac at Spindletop
to hopes & doubts shared on double dates
to that friendship no religion measured up

as Estevan too came to hold that view
even to believing the clergy enslaved
oppressed through blind & dumb obedience
stood firm against its corrupting influence
its fanaticism astonishing to common sense

but saw his colonists bound by law
to profess at least the Catholic faith
to marry by authority of holy church
gave welcome to his friend Muldoon
for in "Paddy" had found a liberal wit

an unwed father who like himself
"looked to Texas as his only home"
his "resting place" & by application for
11 leagues reaffirmed Estevan's belief
in that vain benevolent Irish priest

would like Bill Rabb perform the rite
the one true service Estevan held
made a man devoted to where he lands
to his giving more & craving less
inhabited by a property has invested in

Paddy led by a party to touch his earth
to let it echo him by shouting aloud
pulling its herbs & throwing its stones
taking sweet & bitter into his bones
setting the stakes for surveying him

& though afterwards had come to sell
his deeds outlive mere ownership
for out of such soil his rhyming thrived
words he wrote there surviving still
"The zigzag dart! th' astounding crash!"

"luscious views that expand the heart"
chose the homemade over plagiarism
native flora before any foreign type
prayed that "religious discord fall
And friendship be the creed of all"

nor would ever fail to visit those
jailed in Matamoros or in Mexico
by the cruel & jealous of any day
a Gómez Farías of violent means
threw Wharton into another dungeon

when Muldoon then wouldn't hesitate
to use his office to arrange escape
deception through his cleric's robe
a cassock that padre smuggled in
a consecrated cloth outwitted the guard

George too appearing a deliverer of sorts
in Fort Worth when it all fell through
accused by her parents of needing a shrink
from calling it off & redeeming the ring
taken by him to those hills to recover

neutral ground to the Caddos & Quahpaw
carried their sick & wounded by travois
to the foot of those Ozarks & the curative springs
a million gallons heated daily to fahrenheit 143
George filling the troughs with water & feed

with the dam unwilling the stallion indiscriminately
spilling his seed    spoke of his thoroughbred line
of having had enough of teaching in secondary
would move to Fayetteville for a master's degree
specialize in communications with a major in speech

with his first Nancy then who later proved
unable to bear with his unsettled ways
not his Georgia peach would meet & wed
a cracker to some though none to him
a brain in her class had married young

been deserted just when George arrived
her son adopted & their own to come
when overseas on his tour of duty
training on cabbage for "the gentle way"
returned with a black belt his master gave

moved his family to the pines of Palestine
through distance & crisis keeping in touch
roommates ever by the ties that bind
by rockets still flare & a dog barks on
the errors accepted & the juries hung

a cement holding from that garage apartment
true as well through difference with Andy
patched by that hearing of Scherchen's Mahler
cutting classes for symphonies far more urgent
the listening together there to scherzo & ländler

equally to Count Basie & his "Lil' Darlin'"
his atomic album with Lockjaw's screaming tenor
detonated over & over off those upstairs walls
till the opening chords on Greene's guitar
could set heads straighter than any lecture

Black music for putting a spirit back in
thought history had taken it out of them
by then had surely done its damnedest
yet there they were on & for the record
could enliven not lease a Poplar apartment

at the Co-op found a first Ornette Coleman
on "Congeniality" his white plastic alto sax
seeming to moan "I'm Goin' Tooooo Foat Wuth"
in the Union to catch Bobby Bradford live
those both getting back to Cowtown scales

279

in between on the weekends cleaning it up
when "Momma" Rudin prepared a bohemian meal
wine & candlelight imitating a Puccini scene
celebrated his piece completed for celeste & strings
for the occasion bought another button-down shirt

would buy them too not to do the laundry
too busy composing to bother with *Duz*
his ideas brighter the later at night
sleeping till noon through a major quiz
hoping the absence would somehow wash

the important thing to hear new works
professors mostly sticks-in-the-mud
had gone on repeating or given it up
above all else would learn that lesson
even to flunk would never succumb

from its chest of drawers "Order of Worship"
out its bedroom window "this is just to say"
two strands gathered from that time & place
published by Bracker in *Penny Poems*
in that college paper reviewed by Eckman

had never thought how they'd weave together
could ever make a poetry of a one-block street
going nowhere fast    grown half-persuaded
nothing could come of no Texan no ways
unaware Barker had written around the corner

had Andy to reassure    but not for long
survived German through summer & into fall
then failed a required government departmental
& while he got exempt by his childhood asthma
was classified 1-A at that pre-induction physical

dropped out in dread of draft board Greetings
would go East before they arrived in the mail
would travel ahead of him to New York & Philly
at the latter he'd study under Rochberg at Penn
to record for Nonesuch his electronic flaws

"Hubris" most impressive of those tragic four
his bassless notes whirring higher & higher
then a faint tinkling at the end till it dissipates
like nothing ever suspected existed on Poplar
& yet from that time goes on nourishing still

a pride in one another in spite of dissent
after honest remarks the argument resolved
no sooner expressed than at once regretted
visiting here or there & unable to say it
never wanting to face a pent-up critique

impatiently awaiting the letter to come
response to a latest love discovered or not
to the strain of being stuck with a rotten job
more often from having grown useless & low
when notes or poems went completely ignored

if listened to disliked or condescended
rejected by those in a position to know
made worse when a friend depended upon
had failed to reply by the expected time
cut so by the slightest unsympathetic tone

though still those semesters hold the line
to deliver their mutual remembered message
an assurance spoken in the intimate voice
of those distant sessions held morning & night
convincing yet through disregard & setback

from Philly each would take a separate way
Andy composing in NYC for Nikolai's troupe
to put up with nutty routines of talented Ray
his rebuking when before had humor & dance
& Reck turning abusive & Jordan so distant

whereas on Red River as a trio had formed
with Dave & Roland a Texas Viennese Three
introducing polyrhythms & ragtime tunes
quarter tones in Ives's *Unanswered Question*
how daily sounds could lend a musical speech

though back east just heard as a hick accent
meant misunderstood    meant nothing doing
no work to be had not so much as shoeclerk
ate six bananas with water & walked to enlist
needed three more pounds to pass but didn't

returned to face the inescapable fate
to the isolation of a trying eternal wait
till when it came on that Juneteenth day
seemed against a conscript to discriminate
by exacting in full for that same mistake

"after 200 years' occupation of similar soils
by a free-laboring community" Olmsted wrote
he had never seen "such evidences of waste
as in Texas after 10 years of slavery
How then does it continue?

by constantly borrowing & never paying its debts
the profit of slave labor only obtained
by filching from the nation's capital
from that which the nation owes its posterity
with prohibition would have prospered more rapidly"

from Beaumont to Houston taken by bus
lined up & told Turn your head & cough
but then on insisting their oracle scales
knew well the tale of any underweight
a *deus ex machina* would emancipate

*después* with endearing wit María to conclude
Too bad really    to her had missed out on
reveille    k.p. duty    being ordered around
had made a big difference done loads of good
says Might not have turned out *tan regalón*

let out to enroll at Lamar Tech finished at last
clearing the hurdles with Hagelman's help
beating out Beeson for the Weinbaum prize
glad & yet with his entry much more impressed
so manly so direct & besides it ground an axe

282

wandered with him to Albuquerque & back
to rent here together till hired for September
after checking June to August the Sutton Hall files
for high school openings at its Placement Center
contracted by Superintendent Peay of Hebbronville

to room with Popo & play tennis with Huerta
listening to those *latinos* & imbibing their words
disagreements over thoughts on what they were
Indian Mexican Hispanic full-blood American
welcomed among them as a wetback in reverse

weekends crossed a border in perpetual motion
unending drink for a Gulf cannot be quenched
neither stands nor stops for foreign or national
carries all before it with no sign of preference
a cumulative memory bears along both sides

stopped at Adolfo's home then Nuevo Laredo
for *flautas* & countless *Coronas* dime a bottle
bringing back to Mandy's the *cajeta* in jars
through sand & mesquite through gas & cattle
so-called wastelands yield a special people

in November stunned in an afternoon class
as news came over the school's loudspeaker
a Fort Worth boy hated Dallas more than ever
the first ballot cast & has meant the most
believed bullets ripped him to void that vote

down the road to learn Oswald too attended
sat pen in hand in that Cowtown elementary
in a same wooden seat with stained ink-well
reading the same primers at George C. Clark
on that very playground picked for kickball

in Zapruder's movie through all the smoke
made out shots in front from a raised manhole
saw others fired nearby on that grassy knoll
felt ill then cheated feared Penn Jones' theory
even viewed LBJ in on that vast conspiracy

a cover-up so all-pervasive none untouched
anti-Reds caught up in suspicion's spider web
thinking poisoned by all Jack might have been
his face & cresting hair so refreshingly vigorous
quoting in crisis Milton's "only stand & wait"

had been put off at times by that eastern talk
but would hear it even in the heaviest brogue
"Ich bin" in Boston-Irish at the Berlin wall
where divisions patroled with deadly stare
their weapons still repeating Just you dare

now his Peace Corps goes hardly anywhere
its plumbing lessons aren't found suspect
another capitalist trick to sell the fixtures
the in-fighting continuing after all the tears
over speeches had moved them to volunteer

with spring found a student young & mature
lost her but had instead those Chicano teachers
the consolation of their *tripas* tortilla wrapped
of such sophomores as *Los cuates y Guajalote*
or golf with Jungman a principal firm & fair

& with June came again to Estevan's city
with a bit of that language he learned so well
here to let the seminal room on San Gabriel
two doors down from a couple just newly wed
Gloria a New Braunfels German born & bred

her *Schatzie* Bill the carbon copy of George
neither quite satisfied with whatever they are
two idealists who feel out of place wherever
George jumping from judo to word processor
to the Bayou City's downtown archery trail

its forest land set aside by Jim Hogg's daughter
pot-bellied Governor's statue beside Batts Hall
he a Rusk typesetter shot in the back as a fighter
of corporate lobbyists railroad trusts lynch law
Bill from teacher of history to math to tennis

fed up with each administration & comes on home
a mad Odysseus    George bending his latest bow
to the surprise of Phaiákians & throwing them all
two wives asked to move at a moment's notice
one from Georgia to Palestine to Houston to Palestine

back to Houston while the other from here to Conroe
to Lockhart & back to Conroe    on Bill's hikes to
Guadalupes or Rockies Gloria along or embroiders alone
Nancy letting a gaining-losing hubby's pants out or in
Penelopes to these have added such permanent parts

forever fitting    Bill's epistle to Albuquerque in '69
at the close of that decade when the case came on
for a final Federal hearing    "Notice from last week's
paper that your name is in the headlines
again    Interesting how you maintain

an ambivalent sort of notoriety
Yep, your mug shot made it all the way
to Austin and its daily buttwipe
Seems as though you wrote a letter
critical of the glorious legislature

You realize, of course, that your crime
was not in writing the letter
but in getting it published
I'm writing to tell you how proud I am
Didn't know you still had it in you!

Noticed in the picture that you had some
law books under your arm    Could it mean
you're defending yourself in court?
If you are, remember what Abe Lincoln said
of a man who defends himself—he's a fool

But you already knew that about yourself
One reason your situation caught my attention
was that similar things are happening around here
A teacher was fired from Del Valle High School
where Gloria teaches, because he wore a mustache

285

and didn't wear the right kind of clothes
A visiting speaker to a class in the same school
wasn't allowed to speak because he had long hair
The Land Commissioner ejaculated an edict
that no one who worked for the Land Commission

could wear a skirt higher than the knees
or males wear their sideburns lower
than the top of their earlobe
We lost a city council election to a bunch of red-
necks and ultra-conservatives due to a stupid,

reactionary vote    My God—what's happening?
It's almost as though we're into another McCarthy era
Are we all to lose our rights as citizens
if we don't agree with the so-called establishment?
I'll go to jail first!!!    Gloria sends her greetings to Maria

Hope your kid is alright and doesn't look like you
Maybe we'll see you in Austin sooner now
It's still a pretty town that's worth fighting for
and God knows we need the help    Even poets might
come in handy    So come on back to Texas and prove

that the pen is mightier than the dollar bill
—oops, I mean sword    P.S. Forgot to mention
the guy drove his car at 60 mph through a street
party of hippies    He courteously stopped
and backed over a few more"

in '65 Gloria expecting Becky their first born
still living just off this street in apartments
two blocks down from Barker's home
three from Beeson's last cockroach stand
in front of Federation Club & Neill-Cochran

four from 22nd where they faced Joe Slate's
professor has never bothered to publish a book
just articles with always some exceptional slant
on WCW or Buster Keaton's *What! No Beer?*
confers with his students on an equal footing

hears them out to learn from what they read
in his taste & appetite ranging far & wide
in realms of writing & the silver screen
through food in an Alfred Hitchcock film
to grape-leaf casserole or French cuisine

having found in Patricia his perfect cook
Philadelphian no slipped disk ever holds back
from keeping him company to cavern or beach
her recipes for eggs benedict pastry or bread
satisfying his Sweetish & his wisdom teeth

all happening after having lived on this street
where he woke to two students fenced outside
going at it in the corner lamp's circle of light
at 2 a.m. their clashing foils humorous to him
funny as his landlady Ella Pfluger Pfenning

she disturbed by Whitbread rooming out back
turning up the volume on his operas full blast
subleased & wrote "Low" Joe's favorite poem
both living then across from Faulkner & Hall
the latter a history professor would give no A

to Seals whose average had made the grade
but said he wasn't ready to receive it not yet
Next semester I want you back in this class
at first John would chafe & so resent it
in the end signed up & came away changed

by Silber too who    a student told Slate
had sent her to the east side on a term assignment
credited him she said with her introduction to life
John found him the only man ever to think
being born one-armed a distinct advantage

all coming together on this last river-street
its directory of names gave directions taken
through dictatorial domination & intimidation
those attitudes upsetting either for or against
an earned grade withheld but then outgrown

& there at the other end at twenty-six hundred
right-angled to Poplar where the two streets meet
before a sudden drop-off to pecans & Shoal Creek
his rock home passed how often unready to read
his *Life* of Estevan could have provided a lead

equally Barker's own an example to follow
who in 1894 failed English on the entrance exam
returning to Palestine & that blacksmith shop
to hammer on anvils in the railroad's forge
nights with Shirley Green cramming for grammar

then in '95 to catch the train & try it again
made it through & for his freshman schedule
had English Physics Greek German & French
by '57 all but forgotten    his biographer Pool
after their visit walked by him out to the car

Barker putting around him his grateful arm
thanking him deeply for being so thoughtful
said none of his students had come anymore
could have gone there daily in half a minute
oh to think now how it might have been so

to have met his first or his last seminar
paid attention to a man Duncalf declared
"had he been an Indian had been a chief
looked like one" & Webb who saw it too
said he wore an "unconscious austerity"

or the anonymous sophomore's frank report
furnished him "Standing Bull" as a sobriquet
was thought to possess no more emotion
than the wooden one outside a cigar store
another said was Sioux wrapped in a blanket

to others known as "the Great Stone Face"
a "granite monolith" in his sturdy tweeds
but disturb his class he'd turn bright red
he'd yank those intellectual horn-rims off
& became next thing a 'Frisco earthquake

the productive less praised by him than
generalists "ruminative sympathetic catholic
alert and industrious but not too hurried
to explore the inviting by-paths or to wave
an encouraging greeting" along the way

drove on the links a long straight ball
dealt directly & plainly with one & all
fished the Trinity River & Aransas Bay
once drew in a flounder on a simple hook
if not the first always caught the biggest

on occasion mounted a hobby horse of choice
to champion all subjects as of equal worth
found the arts & sciences hopelessly lost
wandering around with no compass or guide
yielding to every varying fallacious wind

indulging in "unctious elaboration of the obvious"
"his choicest castigation silently reserved for himself"
"half sabre-toothed tiger half St. Francis of Assisi"
"big rough expressive hands" saved a gapped knife
string against a day the Japs shut off the jute supply

could have camped out there to catch a glimpse
of his grim determination & keen grey eye
"tracking down a slanderer of S.F.A."
but arrived at Poplar three years behind
if in time had likely gone unrecognized

Estevan & his fisher of facts    his angler of annals
was oblivious of both as in those Beaumont days
on shopping grocery shelves each week the same
there on Highland Drive at then that Kroger Store
unknowing it looked across to the Bingham home

Mrs. C.W. with humped back & delicate health
how gather hers a mind so nutritious & hale
sought for her scholarship a promising senior
by the serendipity theory of a Prescott Webb
found herself a pitiful budding poet instead

those freshman tuition fees she gladly paid
for the pathetic grades of that first semester
another debt survives this side of the grave
her sacred research performed forever late
even a doctorate unable to communicate

too late too to find his oak-shaded place
once located on this most vital of streets
yet a fact to confirm the poem's design
as Hart Crane learned how Roebling lived
in his very apartment on Columbia Heights

from there the crippled engineer to observe
stringing of cables on his harp-tuned bridge
would sound & cross others to limitless keys
Barker the open sesame to that Mexican cell
through Estevan's *Life* to Poplar & San Gabriel

for hearing the overtones of professors & friends
a voicing made resonant by remembered streams
from Bugbee's beginning down street after street
carried on with reluctance by a sporting Barker
"I had to go on because I had started

As for myself I have always been doubtful
whether a man deserved much credit for doing
a task he wanted above all else to do
there ought to be a record to which men might turn
to realize their unpaid and unpayable obligations"

recalled his wife's weeks in a screenless room
at a Saltillo hotel with not a soul spoke English
through his monotonous study her hardships real
to Beauty too gave something of the measure due
"has lived with me and Austin for all these years"